Teaching Classroom Drama and Theatre

Teaching Classroom Drama and Theatre is all about teaching drama in the modern classroom. The book presents a series of new, exciting and practical units placed in the context of current ideas about classroom practice and presents a new model of how teachers can draw together the various methodologies of process drama and theatre studies. By re-appraising the very different traditions and approaches to drama teaching in schools, it presents examples of integrated projects and lessons suitable for the widest range of teachers and learners. The book is divided into eight units, each focusing on a different theme, which include:

- urban legends
- displaced people
- next stop . . . high school
- the White Rose
- the Mysteries

Each unit provides ideas and lesson plans which can be used as they are or adapted to suit your own particular needs. Each of the different units allows teachers to track student progress and has its own photocopiable resource sheets.

This will be an invaluable resource for anyone who teaches drama in secondary schools or even on a more informal basis. Students training to be teachers will also find this a good source of ideas, as will teacher trainers and mentors.

Martin Lewis is Director of Arts and Assistant Head Teacher at Penketh High School and Specialist Arts College, Warrington.

John Rainer is Subject Leader for Drama within the Institute of Education at Manchester Metropolitan University.

Teaching Classroom Drama and Theatre

Practical projects for secondary schools

Martin Lewis and John Rainer

Routledge
Taylor & Francis Group

LONDON AND NEW YORK

First published 2005
by Routledge
2 Park Square, Milton Park, Abingdon, Oxon OX14 4RN

Simultaneously published in the USA and Canada
by Routledge
270 Madison Ave, New York, NY 10016

Routledge is an imprint of the Taylor & Francis Group

© 2005 Martin Lewis and John Rainer

Typeset in Goudy and Gill Sans
by Keystroke, Jacaranda Lodge, Wolverhampton
Printed and bound in Great Britain
by Bell & Bain Ltd, Glasgow

British Library Cataloguing in Publication Data
A catalogue record for this book is available from the British Library

Library of Congress Cataloging in Publication Data
Lewis, Martin, 1966-
  Teaching classroom drama and theatre : practical projects for
  secondary schools / Martin Lewis and John Rainer.
     p. cm.
  Includes bibliographical references and index.
  ISBN 0–415–31908–0 (pbk. : alk. paper)
  1. Theater–Study and teaching (Secondary)–Handbooks, manuals, etc.
  I. Rainer, John, 1956– II. Title.
  PN2075.L48   2005
  792'.071'2–dc22

ISBN 0–415–31908–0

This book is dedicated to Deborah Farrington, drama teacher, born 13 March 1956, died 13 November 2003.

Contents

Acknowledgements

Thanks to all of our students over the years.

Special thanks to Peter Leach for allowing us to steal some of his play; to Andy Jones who acted as 'consultant editor' in the later stages; to Yvonne Sinclair from the MMU Institute of Education history section; to Anthony Anderson, Documents Librarian, Von KleinSmid Library, University of Southern California for his help; to the Refugee Council and Amnesty International for theirs.

The Toodyay letters are reprinted by permission, courtesy of J. S. Battye Library of West Australian History, accession 564A.

Extracts from *Original Sin* by Peter Leach with music by David Thomas are reprinted by kind permission of the author.

The extract from *Metamorphosis* by S. Berkoff (© the author 1981) is used by kind permission of the original publisher, Amber Lane Press.

The photograph of Jewish people forced to clean streets is © Jewish American Library.

The extract from *The White Rose* by Lillian Garrett-Groag (© the author 1993) is reprinted by permission of the author. All enquiries should be addressed to Peter Hagan, The Gersh Agency, 41 Madison, 33rd Fl., New York NY 10010.

Extracts from the *White Rose* leaflets are from http://www.jlrweb.com/whiterose/leaflets.html

Refugee Council materials are reproduced by permission of the Refugee Council.

The extract from *The Bogus Woman* by Kay Adshead (© the author 2001) reprinted by permission.

Every effort has been made to contact copyright holders and we apologise for any inadvertent omissions. If any acknowledgement is missing it would be appreciated if contact were made care of the publishers so that this can be rectified in any future edition.

Part I

Introduction and rationale

Introduction

Drama is a human need. Throughout time and culture human beings have enacted events in order to understand them or gain power over them. In schools, students and teachers have come to recognise the power and efficacy of drama to simultaneously learn about and create art and culture.

In this book, teachers will find examples of well-researched and carefully resourced projects which attempt to integrate models of drama teaching often seen as separate, or even in opposition. The eight teaching units provide dramas that will engage and motivate a wide range of learners: dramas that are, simply, worth doing. In addition, the dramas provide a vehicle for a structured approach to the explicit teaching of theatrical ideas and concepts. We believe that this is in tune with recent theoretical developments in drama teaching.

Writing this book has led us to seek to re-examine the emphasis and the conceptual basis of our own teaching and we hope that this process might ultimately result in a dynamic, integrated methodology of direct practical use to teachers. Readers who are interested in the theoretical background for this book are referred to the next chapter, where we explore something of the historical context of drama teaching in the UK, and outline the ideas that have informed its writing. For those who wish to 'cut to the chase' and start teaching, we invite you to start exploring the practical units that begin with *Urban Legends*.

Each of the eight teaching units are designed to give very detailed step-by-step guidance to the teachers and workshop leaders facilitating the drama work. However, we would like to stress that the tasks and instructions are not intended to be prescriptive. We hope that teachers and facilitators will make the units their own, tailoring the work to suit the needs and learning styles of their students – and this may well mean wandering 'off-text'! Such departures should be seen as part of the experience of the units. Similarly, the units are designed to enrich, rather than replace any existing curriculum. As the units are comprehensive and fairly substantial in content and length, you can choose to do the whole unit or pick and choose activities as appropriate to your desired outcomes. A brief 'map' of the activities, as well as follow-up evaluation materials which encourage students' reflection and self-assessment, are provided. Each unit has its own photocopiable resource sheets, and its introduction gives an indication of how many lessons the drama work should take to complete. Again, this is provided as a guide, as the timings of lessons and ultimately the project's length will depend upon a group's size, ability and engagement, and the teacher's chosen pathway through the activities.

The third chapter outlines the 'organizing concepts' around which the units are based, and which form the assessment framework. It also provides more detail on how teachers might get the most out of using the book. Grids are provided which allow teachers to track student progress.

We think that you will find the units offer rich learning resources that should lead to memorable drama experiences for your classes and hope that you enjoy teaching them.

Chapter 1

Classroom drama and theatre
A manifesto

I am suggesting that in this coming century we re-educate practitioners to think theatre. If everyone knows that everything they make is theatre then the term may indeed appear more often in titles, but more important than that is the desirability that all teachers would recognise they are sharing the same common ground. All drama courses, all drama activities will be seen as practising one or more theatrical genres. All attempts to weave new theories will have the basic principles of theatre as their shared point of departure.

(Bolton, 2000: 28)

The late 1980s can now be seen as a watershed in relation to the teaching of drama in schools in the UK. At this time two events took place that were to significantly alter the way that drama teachers thought about their subject. The first was the publication of the Education Reform Act, 1988 and the (soon to be discarded) 1989 version of the National Curriculum for England and Wales – which included drama only as a sub-category within English. The second was the publication in 1989 of David Hornbrook's polemical and iconoclastic book, *Education and Dramatic Art.*

It is well-charted territory that the challenges of this period had a profound effect on the drama teaching community. Since then, however, influential writers on school drama have – explicitly or implicitly – responded to Hornbrook's various challenges in a number of ways. Writers such as Jonothan Neelands (1998), John O'Toole (1992), Cecily O'Neill (1995) and Michael Fleming (1994, 1997, 2001) all made attempts to broaden drama teaching's theoretical base and to re-frame 'drama-in-education' or 'process drama' as legitimate *theatre* practice. Gavin Bolton – a practitioner long concerned with exploring the relationship between educational drama and theatre – has also recently and persuasively argued (2000) that a broad conception of theatre should be now be adopted and that this would allow drama in education to be regarded as a legitimate 'sub-genre' of theatre.

By looking to the work of theorists from other fields of enquiry, school drama practitioners during this period began to develop a more *inclusive* conceptual model of practice.

In general terms they attempted to:

- legitimise drama in education (or 'process drama') as a 'sub-genre' of theatre in its own right;
- clarify its relationship to other 'mainstream' theatre genres;
- re-emphasise theatrical outcomes in their teaching, alongside more instrumental aims related to personal and social development and thematic content;
- seek to clarify the *nature* of learning in drama/theatre and explore issues of progression and assessment;
- acknowledge that a drama/theatre curriculum should be *broad and balanced*;
- establish a broad *consensus* of opinion in relation to the above points.

As to the effect of these developments, recent writings on teaching drama have made much reference to an emerging consensus amongst practitioners and the widespread acceptance of 'inclusivity' as its watchword. Although many current teachers would include themselves in this consensus, Mike Fleming, one of the writers who first identified the move 'beyond the fragments' of previous in-fighting and disagreement, has since begun to question what is meant by inclusivity:

> What exactly does an 'inclusive' approach to the subject mean? Does it mean that any form of practice is acceptable? Does consensus mean simply that there is a greater level of tolerance of different approaches, rather than a coherent theoretical rationale or consistent set of practices?
>
> (Fleming, 2001: 2)

What is beyond dispute is that the drama landscape shifted in decisive ways during the 1990s. As a result, drama teachers have sought to re-cast their subject in ways that are having profound effects, not only on what is taught in the name of school drama, but also on how and why it is taught. Some of this 'post-Hornbrook' thinking about drama teaching has influenced our own understanding, and below we identify some key elements.

In an early response to Hornbrook's critique, Stephen Lacey and Brian Woolland (1992) provided an interesting analysis of then-current drama teaching practice in relation to theatre – specifically, what they labelled as 'post-Brechtian modernism'. This interesting article was one of the first explicit attempts to root school drama in a particular *theatrical* tradition. In doing so the authors were consciously seeking to use the conceptual language of theatre to describe a particular example of teaching – in distinction to the assertion that drama in education was somehow outside 'the aesthetic field' (Abbs, in Hornbrook, 1989: ix).

Of particular note in the article were references to the similarities drawn between 'Brechtian' acting and the drama teaching technique of *teacher in role*. Previous assumptions about role-playing had largely taken it to be qualitatively different to 'acting', but Woolland and Lacey were able to point persuasively to conceptual similarities. Although Gavin Bolton (1998) has recently explored the nature of classroom acting in some detail, others have looked to other traditions for theoretical models which would help to clarify this and other relationships. In our own work we have been increasingly drawn to the work of contemporary practitioners consciously operating in a radical 'art theatre' tradition.

In his book *A Formalist Theatre*, Michael Kirby helpfully frames the issue of what is meant by *acting* in terms of the contemporary theatre's 'flight' from naturalism:

> As recently as the fall and winter of 1964 the Tulane Drama Review devoted two complete issues to Stanislavski; now the method no longer has the absolute dominance it once did in this country, and certain alternative approaches have attracted great interest. Everyone now seems to realise that 'acting' does not mean just one thing – the attempt to imitate life in a realistic and detailed fashion.
>
> (Kirby, 1987: 14)

He also makes interesting observations about the general changes occurring in contemporary theatre practice which seem to resonate with the concerns of school drama:

> [E]very aspect of theatre in this country [the US] has changed [since the 1960s]: scripts have lost their importance and performances are created collectively; the physical relationship between audience and performance has been altered in many different ways and has been made an inherent part of the piece; audience participation has been investigated; 'found' spaces rather than theatres have been used for performance . . . there has been an increased emphasis on movement and on visual imagery . . .
>
> (Ibid.: 14–15)

Kirby also provides a useful 'continuum of acting behaviours' in which he attempts to classify acting within a broader context of performance:

Acting can be said to exist in the smallest and simplest action that involves pretence.

(Ibid.: 7)

Kirby's continuum of 'acting behaviours' provides a taxonomy which can be applied to all performance contexts from 'not acting' at all, through 'simple' to more 'complex' forms of acting. Interestingly, he also suggests that contemporary theatre has seen a shift away from the 'complex' end of the continuum, towards simpler, perhaps less naturalistic styles of performance. Viewed in this perspective 'role play', commonly encountered in educational contexts, is clearly a form of acting, and may legitimately be seen alongside other forms of contemporary theatre practice. Kirby's analysis of non-naturalistic acting allows a number of classroom practices – including that of *teacher in role* – to find *theatrical* legitimacy. Within Kirby's framework, role-playing can be seen as consonant with the notion of 'simple' acting; neither less, nor more legitimate as 'art' than other forms.

Other writers have looked even further afield. Hamish Fyfe, for instance, advocates that drama teachers seek to 'broaden the base' of their subject by looking to the work of anthropologists:

As well as offering a potential synthesis of theatre practice anthropology presents a number of challenges for those involved in theatre and education. These challenges occur because it addresses the role, function and nature of drama within a total cultural context as opposed to the relatively narrow educational sphere.

(Fyfe, 2001: 42)

In this vein, the work of Richard Schechner (1985, 1988, 1993) and Eugenio Barba (1994) in the field of theatre anthropology – has helped to contextualise the cultural hegemony of Euro-American commercial and art theatre traditions within a wider field of world performance genres. In their research they have examined the functions of theatre in a wide range of cultural contexts. A particularly helpful notion associated with this perspective is that of *efficacy* – that theatre is culturally 'useful' in various ways. Again, this idea challenges the Eurocentric assumption – made by Peter Abbs and others associated with Hornbrook's critique – that theatre used *for a purpose* is somehow outside the aesthetic domain.

Drawing on this work, drama educationalists such as Neelands (1994) have promoted a broader re-examination of drama-in-education and advocated that it be re-constituted as a legitimate, specialised theatre sub-genre alongside others (Theatre in Education, drama therapy, youth theatre, community theatre, etc.). Interestingly, at the same time, theatre academics working in the 'mainstream' of university drama departments have also moved the conceptual boundaries of their own discipline: the term 'applied theatre', used in an inclusive manner, has wide currency in the UK and abroad as an umbrella term for a wide range of efficacious practice:

[Applied theatre is] . . . theatre removed from a traditional (perhaps building-based) context and applied to the objectives of wider social institutions, organisations and agencies. The term 'theatre' is used to include all those processes, techniques, approaches and skills that are in any way components of drama practice. This may be scripted performance, participatory workshops, a single moment of role play, or an extended rehearsal sequence.

(Thompson, 1999: 9)

Interestingly, Thompson also acknowledges the ambiguous and sometimes turbulent relationship between theatre practice of this kind and the host 'agency'. His comments will be recognised by all school drama teachers who have seen their subject as a form of cultural – as well as educational – intervention:

Theatre approaches interact with an agency's objectives, sometimes to fulfil them, sometimes to extend them, and occasionally to undermine them. Theatre's contact is with the audience or participants first, and the social institution second . . . The application of theatre may fit snugly, or it may grate, it may become an easy complement or a point of friction. An extended use of creative role play in the classroom may be rewarding for the young people, but come into conflict with the tight objectives of a pre-set curriculum.

(Ibid.: 10)

Another aspect in the development of thinking about drama practice has been the questioning of hierarchical models deriving from what has been described as a 'cultural heritage' position. In the cultural heritage model (Fleming, 2001), perhaps most clearly expressed in the Arts Councils' publications on drama (1992, 2003), drama work with young people in schools is clearly seen as existing at the base of a hierarchy, with 'proper theatre' as represented by the 'creative industries' – perhaps the Royal Shakespeare Company or the National Theatre – at the apex. In efforts to challenge a view of theatre which uncritically foregrounds some institutions and practices, much recent work – drawing on Schechner's anthropological approach – has sought to emphasise the context and function of different traditions of theatre, and crucially of drama teaching itself, by establishing a parallel rather than hierarchical model; not 'better', just *different* (Neelands, 1994).

Others, such as John O'Toole (1992), have emphasised the negotiated, participatory and 'processual' nature of drama-in-education and have highlighted conceptual similarities present in other examples of theatre practice across time and culture. O'Toole has also pointed out that the interchangeability of the roles of 'actor', 'audience' or 'director' in different cultural forms of theatre have clear similarities to the role flexibility found in classroom drama: his work helpfully reminds us that the notion that these roles should be fixed and performed by separate, 'professionalised' groups of people is true of only certain cultural traditions of theatrical production – most notably in the Western theatre of the last 300 or so years (O'Toole, 1992: 185).

In particular, O'Toole cites the work of Augusto Boal as an example of theatre practice in some ways analogous to drama work in schools. Interestingly, during the 1980s and 1990s (at the same time that the practice of the drama educator Dorothy Heathcote was under attack), the work of Augusto Boal – also working in improvised, participatory and highly 'processual' forms, but within a self-consciously theatrical tradition – was establishing itself within university theatre departments. In our work tutoring and mentoring post-graduate trainee teachers of drama – themselves the product of university theatre degree courses in the UK – we have found universal acceptance of the legitimacy of participatory theatre forms due to their familiarity with the highly context-specific work of Boal. This does at least give us a point of conceptual contact, but students are often surprised by the comparative sophistication and theatrical potency of the practice found in good secondary school drama departments. It may be interesting to speculate why these other participatory and emancipatory theatre practices – also context bound, but within the somewhat less rarified world of the school classroom – have not found such legitimacy within those same universities.

Within the school drama curriculum in recent years, and in spite of its critics, we have seen the wide acceptance of process-oriented approaches to drama teaching based on the drama-in-education model. It is true to say, however, that in many schools teachers have been keen to ensure that their process-based work has been balanced with more explicitly theatrical teaching. Interestingly, this, combined with the broader theoretical base of many recently trained drama teachers, has had the effect that process-based work now often appears as one separate element of a much wider drama curriculum. Neelands has stressed the importance of balancing work emphasising the theatrical 'literary and private' mainstream of school English and theatre studies with drama rooted in an 'oral and communal' tradition (Neelands, 1998: 23). This alternative tradition, which is described as participatory and learner-centred, is seen as providing a balance for drama teaching rooted in more conventionally academic literary and theatrical concerns. In this tradition, Neelands' 'convention-led' teaching is seen as an alternative set of practices derived from children's play, storytelling, and the cultural forms which bind and challenge communities – including schools. Neelands has emphasised the importance of context in defining the particular balance of drama taught, so that schools and teachers might define the approach best suited to the community of learners they serve. In doing so, the work of Neelands rightly attempts to reach out to drama teachers rooted in all traditions.

However, whilst the overall effect of these developments in thinking about drama has been to legitimise the 'process' tradition of drama teaching, we believe that one worrying – and para-doxical – outcome could be its *ghettoisation*. In school drama curriculum statements both in the UK and further afield it is now not unusual to see 'process drama' included as a 'theme' or unit of work alongside others more explicitly oriented towards 'traditional' theatre ('melodrama'; 'soap opera'; 'Brecht'). In some schools, work on 'process' is now somewhat confusingly separated from the 'more serious' theatrical emphasis found in other units of work. One example of this approach is a recent textbook that includes a single chapter utilising 'role play' in an approach to storytelling, before the book moves on to seemingly more rarified work on 'physical theatre', 'performing scripted plays' and 'teaching theatre practitioners', amongst other topics (Nicholson, 2000). The explicitly theatrical work described in the book does, of course, also depend upon a pedagogical 'process' in order to become accessible to learners, whether or not this is acknow-ledged. Regardless of the editor's intention, the potential effect is to marginalise one tradition of practice. In this book 'role play' is relegated to a tool only useful in exploring 'storytelling'.

However, it is clear that where emphasis is on the explicit teaching and learning of theatre, as in Hornbrook's arbitrary suggestions for a key stage three curriculum (1998b), teachers overlook the pedagogical and methodological processes involved in making the work *accessible* to students at their peril. In the training of secondary drama teachers in the UK there has been much recent emphasis placed on the acquisition of high levels of 'subject knowledge'. A key realisation of those involved in the training process has been that a high level of 'subject knowledge' of theatre on the part of the teacher does not in itself guarantee quality theatrical learning on the part of pupils. As many teachers know, when their intentions are consciously theatrical it is *especially* important to provide 'structure' in order to make complex and abstract ideas accessible to the widest range of learners. It has long been observed that, importantly, where a tradition of process work has been strong in a particular school, performance work has been richer as a result. We believe that an understanding of theatrical forms and processes can be best approached through the concrete and practical classroom tradition of drama teaching that has evolved to suit the needs of learners over the last 50 years. It is a tradition that rightly takes account of personal and social learning, of language development and cultural context, of content, as well as form. Rooting our work in this tradition has, paradoxically, enabled us to turn our attention to ways of making learning about theatre and performance more explicit – in a *classroom theatre*.

This book is therefore an attempt to:

- give teachers the means to teach and explore theatrical concepts without losing the essentially student-centred, process-oriented and participatory character of the best drama teaching;
- provide the means to make this agenda explicit and open to students;
- suggest that an emphasis on methodology and 'process' is a crucial element in making such learning about theatre accessible;
- provide frameworks for lessons where the skills and concepts explored in this *classroom theatre* will be learned within the context of significant content which is relevant and interesting to learners;
- offer another interpretation of the notion of an *inclusive* or, more accurately, an *integrated* drama curriculum.

In trying to reclaim the language of theatre for the classroom we have, of course, created for ourselves some interesting definitional problems. Conventionally, the term 'drama' refers to the school subject, but is also used as a generic term and as a noun denoting a dramatic artwork. In conventional usage, the term 'theatre' is most often used to describe those specific practices that relate to formal performance to an audience. In asserting that the practice found in school classrooms (which appears as 'drama' on every school timetable) is a form of *theatre* we run the risk of terminological inconsistency if we defer to conventional usage. However, for the sake of clarity of meaning we hope that readers will put up with some inconsistency. The alternative – to refer to theatre/drama throughout the text – is unappealing, and equally inconsistent! Ironically, and after long discussion, we have included the word 'drama' in the title of this book so as to avoid alienating potential readers – which proves our point! As Gavin Bolton suggests, perhaps in the future the term 'theatre' will be able to be applied to a school subject without divisive connotations.

The units that follow in Section 2 are not intended to be blueprints for practice. Although we do provide detailed accounts of particular projects, we hope that teachers will select the elements of the work that best suit their intentions, and that students will find a sense of ownership and increasing autonomy as the work progresses.

Chapter 2

Teaching the units
Rationale and assessment

Throughout the book we assume that, in order to develop and become autonomous practitioners in drama, students will need:

- personal and social abilities;
- performance skills;
- knowledge and understanding of theatrical ideas and concepts.

It is also assumed that particular drama students in a cohort or group will possess aspects of these abilities in different measure. It could be, for instance, that a particular student might have moderate performance skills, but has outstanding ability to visualise, shape and plan drama with their peers. We believe that students will only begin to work to their full potential when they have acquired a balance of all three of these core elements and one task of the effective drama teacher is to identify individual strengths and areas for development, and to provide students with opportunities to extend their skills and understanding across the spectrum that leads to making effective classroom theatre.

Personal and social abilities

These are necessary in order to make drama because of the social, co-operative nature of the art form. Teachers will be aware that classes or groups of students with poor 'social health' will be severely inhibited in their ability to make effective drama. In many ways these abilities are prerequisites to good drama, but the process of making and responding critically to drama does itself provide a fertile environment within which students can practise these skills. The personal and social aspect of classroom work consists of interactive skills – teamwork, negotiation and problem solving, as well as the ability to contribute ideas and critical evaluation to the process of making theatre. It also includes abilities such as empathy, as well as a range of 'thinking skills'.[1]

Performance skills

Performance skills are needed in order to make students' ideas concrete. To participate in a process of dramatic exploration and to turn plans and possibilities into drama, individual students will need to develop and draw upon a wide range of skills. Included in this category are physical and vocal skills, as well as technical abilities relating to design, stage management and theatre technology.

Knowledge and understanding of theatrical ideas and concepts

The third strand to the framework will underpin students' ability to make drama or present it to an audience.

Worthwhile work in the classroom will depend upon students' ability to apply their knowledge of theatre ideas and concepts in practice. Besides practical skills, therefore, students will also need to develop a wide range of knowledge and understanding of the form and language of theatre. It is obviously important that we are explicit about the nature of the theatrical learning we are aiming to develop in our students.

Organising concepts

The organising theatrical concepts explored through the units in this book are grouped into seven broad categories. The categories are not intended to be inclusive or complete, but rather are general headings intended to help organise and 'construct' students' conceptual knowledge of theatre:

Role

- Role and character.
- Simple and complex acting.
- Stereotypes, archetypes and stock characters.

Previous writers about drama have often emphasised 'role-taking' as the central activity in drama, highlighting the participant's active engagement in exploring fictional situations from another's perspective or point of view. Many have also sought to differentiate between 'role-playing' and 'acting', assuming that acting is concerned only with the representation of 'rounded' characters.[2] However, rather than attempt to make rigid distinctions between such terms as 'role' and 'character' it seems more appropriate to differentiate between different kinds of acting behaviours, appropriate to different forms of theatre. In the units, opportunities are given for students to explore different aspects of role and character, and to begin to place different kinds of acting behaviours into their theatrical context. By working through the units they will also begin to understand the use of stereotypes, archetypes and stock characters and relate this work to a variety of theatre forms.

Form

- Signs, symbols and metaphors.
- Realism and stylisation.
- Genre and style.
- Ritual.

Concepts related to theatrical form are introduced through active theatre making that will help students recognise formal elements in their work and the work of others. Some time is spent exploring the use of signs, symbols and metaphors in theatre. However, care will be taken to avoid the fragmented approach to responding to drama sometimes found in books advocating semiotic forms of analysis. All of the work found in this book is aimed at engaging students in theatrical ideas through the active exploration of significant content, and encouraging both affective and more cognitive responses. It also aims to help them to find appropriate forms for their own responses to this content. Beginning with exploring broad distinctions between realism and stylisation, the book will enable students to understand aspects of *genre* and *style* in their work and the work of others, as well as investigate the use of *ritual* elements.

Structure

- Narrative and plot.
- Drama conventions as structural elements.
- The manipulation of time and place – linear and non-linear structure.
- Narrative voices.
- Non-narrative structures – documentary and montage.

Throughout the units some time is spent enabling students to experiment with various techniques that will help them to recognise structural elements in drama and use them to enhance their own work. A basic understanding of *drama conventions* (Neelands, 2000) and the distinction between *narrative* and *plot* will become a starting point for examining how *time* and *place* is manipulated in drama. From a simple *linear structure*, techniques such as *flashback and cross-cutting* will enable students to include more structural sophistication in their work, and will allow them to use both *narrative* and *non-narrative structures* – such as *montage*. They will also examine the dramatic potential of different *narrative voices*, selected for their particular dramatic effect.

Stage

- Performer and audience relationships.
- Space.
- Movement and body language.
- Design elements.

In seeking to integrate performative and experiential traditions of drama teaching, this book is not a performance handbook. Nevertheless, certain units do enable students to develop understanding and skills in relation to stage elements.

Performer and audience relationships and different forms of staging are investigated, as is a more general consideration of how the manipulation of *space* helps create meaning (*proxemics*), and the importance of movement and body language. How light and sound and other design elements might be utilised to enhance performance work is also considered – but, as always, within the context of active participation in drama.

Text

- Improvisation, composition and performance.
- Stage and media texts.
- Script notation and performance.
- Subtext and interpretation.

The interrelation of the central concepts of improvisation, composition and performance in drama production processes is seen as central to this aspect of the book. An understanding of *script conventions* in conventionally notated drama will lead students into a consideration of aspects such as *subtext*, and through an understanding of stage and media texts the notion of script as a basis for performance – within which actors and directors *interpret* the writer's plan – will be practically explored.

Audience

- The societal functions of drama.
- Focus, tension and release.
- Audience response.

The concept of *audience* and its active role in the making of meaning will provide students with an introduction to key concepts related to some of the societal functions of drama. The notion of performance efficacy will be introduced through practical work on dramas variously intended to entertain, inform and challenge the audience. How different forms of drama seek to 'position' the audience, and how audiences experience drama through moments of *focus, tension and release* will also be explored.

Content

- Form, content and meaning.
- History and fiction.

How meaning in drama is created through the integration of *form* and *content* is a theme that runs throughout all of the units. As a number of the units are based on historical material, issues related to the dramatisation of 'facts' and the testimony of real people will be examined.

In practice, because the book is organised thematically, students' understanding of these central concepts will not be developed in a linear way. Although the units in the book are identified in terms of progression, the concepts themselves are often revisited in a number of units. We believe that this accurately represents how students actually learn in drama. It may be helpful to remind ourselves of the guiding principles of progression suggested by the National Curriculum Council in its 1990 report, *The Arts 5–16, A Curriculum Framework*, and recently adapted by the New Zealand Ministry of Education:

- *Complexity*: issues dealt with by younger students can be revisited with older students in more complex and sophisticated ways.
- *Control*: students should acquire increasing control of the means of dramatic expression of the forms that drama takes.
- *Depth*: students move from a broad range of drama experiences to exploring individual projects in more depth.
- *Independence*: students become increasingly autonomous.

These four principles are helpful in describing pupil progression in broad terms, whilst also capturing something of the 'spiral' nature of learning in the subject and they have served as our guide throughout this project.

Assessment

An integrated curriculum demands that a wide range of learning outcomes might be legitimately considered. Eisner (1994) reminds us of the need to include *expressive* as well as *behavioural* objectives in our work. The drive towards assessment-driven curriculae in recent years has tended to foreground the measurable and predicted outcomes of educational processes, at the expense of the unpredictable or serendipitous. This process, Eisner reminds us, tends to limit and distort the potential of students' learning in the arts.

Behavioural objectives relate to the specific 'behaviours' we expect students to demonstrate in order to judge that learning has taken place. For example, students may demonstrate how they are able to restructure a linear narrative into a dramatic plot by manipulating time through the use of flashback techniques.

Expressive objectives, on the other hand, grow out of the students' encounter with the learning context, and assume that it is desirable to provide educational experiences that produce unspecified outcomes. For example, students may have highly personal empathetic responses to the issues explored in a drama about asylum seekers: their consciousness of the plight of refugees arising from this drama may alter their own perspective on the issue. It is inappropriate to attempt to 'assess' such expressive outcomes. Such outcomes are, nonetheless, valid forms of learning.

In the units in this book we attempt to balance more structured behavioural objectives in relation to students' *progress* in drama with the unpredictable, but valuable, outcomes which come as a result of the *quality* of students' encounters with the content of the work. Students' engagement with artistic experiences of all kinds may well lead to unexpected outcomes of this nature. It is perhaps a sign of the hegemonic pressures operating in schools that even teachers of the arts have come to distrust such objectives as legitimate and valuable outcomes of their work. Paradoxically, experience suggests that drama teaching that lacks this balance – of structured and unstructured, predicted and unpredictable, safety and risk-taking – can be arid and uninspiring.

As stated earlier, students' ability in drama depends upon knowledge and understanding of theatrical concepts as well as the balance of individual and group skills necessary to apply this knowledge in practice. In terms of assessment, we believe that it is only feasible to assess the products of students' efforts – what students make, do, say or write. Evidence of their skills and knowledge will therefore be found in their practical drama, and what they say or write about drama (see Figure 1).

Making and performing

A student's ability to *make* effective drama will depend upon his or her social abilities, performance skills and their understanding of theatrical ideas. In practice in the classroom, evidence of a student's achievements in *making* drama will usually be provided through its *performance* – in formal, or less formal, contexts. In the modern drama classroom – and in the type of work we advocate in this book – students are constantly and fluidly moving between the *making* and *performance* of drama. Work is developed through a range of creative processes and is constantly 'performed' as *part* of the process of creation and appraisal. In some cases it is redrafted or refined, and an 'end product' may emerge which is presented more formally, but conceptually it is difficult to separate out these elements in order to make assessment valid. In any case, work that is rehearsed and performed to an audience, no matter how formal, is not 'fixed' and continues to be 'remade' each time it is performed.

In this kind of work, attempting to employ different sets of assessment criteria for the processes of making drama to those used to assess its performance will lead to categoric confusion – such as that found in much recent writing about assessment in drama in the UK. For instance, in the framework suggested by Arts Council England in the second edition of their publication *Drama in Schools* (2003) the following criteria are found within the *Performing* strand of a conventional three-strand (making; performing; responding) assessment model:

> (Pupils can)
> . . . act out *improvised* dramas . . . *creating* characters that are clearly different from themselves . . .
>
> (level three)
>
> . . . *organise* a short, clear and coherent performance for an audience . . .
>
> (level five)
>
> . . . *refine* their work in rehearsal, develop a piece of devised work and *transcribe* it into a scripted scene.
>
> (level seven)
> (Arts Council England, 2003: 32–41; our emphasis)

All of these processes (*improvising, creating, organising, refining, transcribing*) are clearly activities related to the *making* of drama; evidence that they have taken place will certainly be found in its performance, but the processes themselves, identified as criteria for assessment within the *performance* strand, are arguably not performance-related criteria at all. Similar confusions are to be found in other publications advocating a three-strand assessment model. In particular, the improvised basis of much classroom drama and the fluid movement between *creating* drama and

The assessment process

In order to be good at drama students need to acquire...

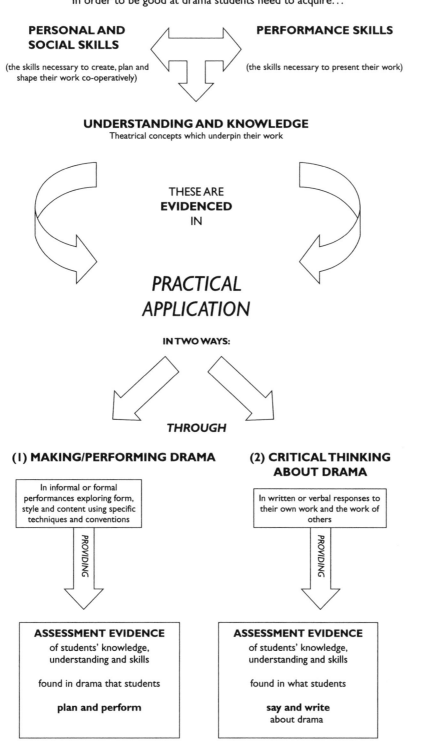

PERSONAL AND SOCIAL SKILLS

(the skills necessary to create, plan and shape their work co-operatively)

PERFORMANCE SKILLS

(the skills necessary to present their work)

UNDERSTANDING AND KNOWLEDGE
Theatrical concepts which underpin their work

THESE ARE
EVIDENCED
IN

PRACTICAL
APPLICATION

IN TWO WAYS:

THROUGH

(1) MAKING/PERFORMING DRAMA

In informal or formal performances exploring form, style and content using specific techniques and conventions

PROVIDING

ASSESSMENT EVIDENCE

of students' knowledge, understanding and skills

found in drama that students

plan and perform

(2) CRITICAL THINKING ABOUT DRAMA

In written or verbal responses to their own work and the work of others

PROVIDING

ASSESSMENT EVIDENCE

of students' knowledge, understanding and skills

found in what students

say and write
about drama

performing it found in practice in many classrooms creates much confusion. For instance, Kemp and Ashwell (2000) suggest a categoric distinction between 'working supportively and creatively with others' and 'working supportively and creatively with others *in performance*' (our emphasis), providing different sets of criteria for both strands. Besides being difficult to apply in practice, an effect of this is to force a distinction between 'informal' performance (for instance, of work in progress, or within a 'process drama') and formal performance 'for a public audience'. In our view, rigid conceptual distinctions of this kind are unhelpful. As in so many conceptual problems of this kind, a *continuum* – in this case from 'formal' to 'informal' performance – is a much more accurate description of what is actually found in practice. This continuum might range from a school drama company playing at a drama festival or competition, or devised or scripted drama presented to an external examiner (arguably the only truly 'public' audiences likely to be encountered by most school students) through school plays performed to largely sympathetic audiences of parents and friends, to inter-form presentations, to the many moments in drama lessons where work is presented to each other and to the teacher. At what point in the continuum should the 'working together in performance' criteria be judged to apply? Is it logical that one set of criteria apply only to the first two or three examples, and different criteria apply to the others?

The problems inherent in separating criteria for *making* from those for *performing* are further exacerbated if one considers the notion common in music education that true improvisation – commonly employed in classroom work in the form of role play or 'spontaneous improvisation' – is actually '*composition through performance*'. This is clearly true of the jazz musician, action painter or contemporary dancer improvising; conceptually it is equally true of the student improvising in a classroom drama – this 'composition through performance' could just as easily be transcribed and notated. Strictly speaking, therefore, using a conventional three-strand assessment model, classroom improvisation, as well as the informal classroom presentation of such 'composed' devices as tableaux, should be judged using the criteria put aside for *performance*. This is clearly not the authors' intention!

For these reasons we do not divide *making* and *performing* into separate assessment strands: in attempting to *integrate* process and performance traditions of drama teaching we see no reason to reinforce this false and somewhat confusing distinction. Instead we combine *making/performing* as a single assessment strand. (For a further discussion of this issue see Fleming, 2001: 65–73.)

When assessing presentations of pupils' work:

- To what extent does the work presented provide evidence of understanding of dramatic ideas?
- To what extent does it provide evidence of individual performance skills?
- To what extent are the co-operative and interactive skills of group members evidenced?

Critical responses

Other evidence of a student's learning will be found in their critical responses to drama:

- To what extent do students' written or oral statements about drama provide evidence of their understanding of theatrical ideas and concepts?
- What insight does it give about their performance skills or personal and social abilities?

Tracking progress

Some previous attempts to provide assessment and progression grids to track student progress in drama, although helpful conceptually, have proved difficult to operate in practice. If one aim of assessment is to track students' progress against their previous attainment – in an *ipsative* process – it is imperative that the process of assessment itself is practical enough to be applied at regular intervals. On a slightly less pragmatic level, rigid assessment schemes can have the tendency to distort the drama curriculum itself by reinforcing a normative and linear account of learning.

The emphasis on the development of pupils' conceptual learning in drama found in this book does not assume a simple relationship between curriculum delivery and student learning. Instead, it suggests a cumulative process within which students continually revisit conceptual categories to 'construct' their own increasingly sophisticated 'map' of the theatrical terrain. Therefore, rather than specify the age of the students (or the particular school term in which the unit is to be taught) we provide broad bands of progression and leave it to teachers to judge what is most suitable for their students. This will depend not only upon the students' age and ability but also upon their previous experience of drama, as well as the dynamics found within a particular group and the students' general levels of confidence. Within the units, a range of possible tasks and activities are provided and teachers are encouraged to use their judgement to select those most appropriate for their classes.

We identify the intended learning outcomes for each unit of work in terms of theatrical knowledge and skills, but assume that teachers will be able to vary their delivery of particular tasks in order to emphasise opportunities for personal and social learning appropriate to the particular class.

Unlike some other assessment schemes, which are principally addressed to teachers, the emphasis here is on the student, through self- and peer assessment, and to that end we provide a framework that is intended to help students identify their own progress, and to open a dialogue with their teacher. The framework identifies progression in three areas:

1   Conceptual knowledge and understanding.
2   Personal and social learning.
3   Performance skills.

In area one – *conceptual knowledge and understanding* – we provide two assessment grids. One offers an overview of learning opportunities in this area and is provided for teachers (pages 19–20), and the other is designed for self-assessment by students (pages 21–22). There is also a record sheet for students to complete (page 23).

In area two – *personal and social learning* – the following criteria can be applied when gathering evidence of students' abilities:

To what extent is the student able to:

- contribute to group discussion or planning;
- participate in problem-solving and decision making;
- co-operate to plan and present drama;
- negotiate with others in initiating, accepting and shaping ideas;
- adapt their approach in order to work with a range of peers?

We also present a matrix that enables students to identify their own contribution to the group work they have completed (see the 'Group skills audit' pages 24–25).

The final set of criteria help to focus the teacher on students' *performance skills* within the context of their practical drama work. Performance skills can, of course, be evidenced in improvised dramas and informal classroom presentations, as well as in more formal performances:

- appropriate use of vocal skills in characterisation or in the creation of setting, mood and atmosphere;
- application of appropriate physical or gestural expression to enhance the drama;
- the ability to shape a drama spontaneously, as it unfolds;
- the ability to maintain focus and concentration;
- the ability to sustain role using appropriate language and physicality;

- awareness of the importance of pace and timing;
- the ability to communicate ideas and intentions to an audience.

As students' learning in drama can only be evidenced through the products of their work, we encourage teachers and students to seek evidence of progress in the work that has been produced – first through the presentation of practical work, and second in relation to students' critical responses to their work.

In order to help teachers and students to appraise the particular outcomes for each unit we also provide a proforma, which again is intended to involve students in the process through peer- and self-assessment (pages 26–28). At the end of each unit, students are asked to respond to a range of prompts and tasks, as well as to engage in reflective writing about the unit (a list of suggested questions is given on page 29). This material works in support of the teacher's own ongoing assessments, and teachers can then develop the information collated into more detailed formative – or indeed summative – feedback for students. The whole process is designed to let students gain access to the loop of assessment from which all too often they are excluded.

The assessment process therefore aims:

- to help students to identify what they know and can do and, crucially, what they can do to progress further;
- to provide teachers with feedback data to make their teaching more effective.

Identifying progression 'levels' in isolation does not improve students' learning: weighing something does not make it heavier!

Focus

Drama is a complex process. From the range of assessment materials, we urge teachers to focus on applying a manageable range of criteria at any one assessment point. Over time, a range of information can be accumulated, and this will ensure that the assessment process remains manageable, whilst providing teachers and pupils with useful information.

Notes

1 There has been much recent interest in 'thinking skills' or cognitive acceleration programmes based on drama activities. See, for example, Wigan LEA (2002).
2 For a further discussion of this issue in the context of a drama lesson, see Unit 2.

Conceptual knowledge and understanding assessment grid (teacher version)

Level 1	Level 2	Level 3
Working towards . . . **ROLE** Understands that taking on a role is a basic element of drama and that it allows the exploration of situations and ideas from another's perspective or point of view. Is aware of naturalistic forms of acting, but may assume that verisimilitude equals quality, leading to an over-reliance upon 'realistic' portrayals.	Working towards . . . **ROLE** Understands and differentiates between role and character as simple and more complex forms of acting. There is an emerging awareness of a range of styles, including more stylised approaches.	Working towards . . . **ROLE** Understands that there are many different forms of acting, from simple role taking through stereotypes, stock characters and archetypes to complex naturalistic characterisations. Understands that acting style is fundamentally linked to particular theatrical styles or genres.
Working towards . . . **FORM** Is becoming aware of a range of conventions and can apply these forms to express their own ideas. Can recognise the difference between naturalistic and stylised or abstract drama, mainly by identifying the simple sign system or iconography of different theatrical styles. They may have experienced in their own work elements of ritual and stylisation, but may not necessarily relate this to other practitioners or genres.	Working towards . . . **FORM** Can select and discriminate between appropriate techniques and conventions from an increasingly wide range in order to bring form to their ideas. Can recognise the characteristics of a wide range of theatre styles and genres and is able to explain the theatrical conventions that govern some theatre forms with which they are familiar.	Working towards . . . **FORM** Can make sophisticated choices in finding appropriate dramatic forms to dramatise own ideas, and can justify these decisions. Has a developing understanding of a range of different theatrical genres and styles. Understands how different theatre styles use particular signs, symbols and metaphors to communicate meaning. Understands how meaning in drama is created through the integration of form and content. Has an emerging awareness of the social and historical context of some theatre forms.
Working towards . . . **STRUCTURE** Can recognise basic structural elements in drama and is aware of differences in structure between different kinds of drama. In own work can plan straightforward linear narratives. With teacher's intervention will be able to use drama conventions in order to manipulate time and place and vary the structure of their work. Will be aware of the basic difference between narrative and plot.	Working towards . . . **STRUCTURE** Can use and manipulate structural elements when planning dramas of their own. Can demonstrate the difference between narrative and plot by identifying key moments and manipulating time and space in their work – using montage, juxtaposition, cross-cutting or circular plot structures.	Working towards . . . **STRUCTURE** Will be aware of a wide range of structural possibilities in different genres of drama. Will be skilful at manipulating structural elements when planning dramas of their own. Will be able to structure episodic drama that is organised through themes rather than through the manipulation of time. Can create effective non-narrative structures as well as employing different narrative voices and identifying their functions.
Working towards . . . **STAGE** Will have some understanding of how stage and design elements can contribute to the meaning of a drama. Will be aware of a limited range of stage conventions and have some understanding of the possible range of performer/audience relationships. Will have some understanding of how the use of space creates meaning.	Working towards . . . **STAGE** Can demonstrate the use of different kinds of staging, and is aware of some of the consequent differences in audience/performer relationships. Is able to demonstrate how design elements can enhance the meaning of the drama.	Working towards . . . **STAGE** Is aware of a wide range of possible audience/performer relationships and can give examples from their own work and the work of others. Has a clear understanding of how manipulating the *mise-en-scène* – the whole stage picture – can create subtle nuances in meaning.

continued

Teacher version continued

Level 1	Level 2	Level 3

Working towards . . .

TEXT
Will understand that text is a broad term that does not just relate to scripted drama, and that improvisation can be a form of composition. Will be able to demonstrate how written, visual and aural texts of various kinds can be used to stimulate drama. Will be aware that play scripts are just one means of notating drama performance and will have an emerging understanding of script conventions. With guidance, will be able to explore and interpret a range of scripts.

Working towards . . .

TEXT
Can respond to a range of written, visual and aural texts identifying significant features and dramatic potential. Has an understanding of script conventions across a range of genres, and can use the scripts as a basis for performance and interpretation by actors and directors.

Working towards . . .

TEXT
Will understand the interrelationship between improvisation, composition and performance. Will be aware of a wide range of methods to create a dramatic text. Will be able to interpret a range of texts with sensitivity and skill, drawing out subtextual elements.

Working towards . . .

AUDIENCE
Will understand that audience is a key element in drama, and that theatre is a communicative process. Will have a basic understanding of how different kinds of drama intend different effects, and create different relationships with their audience.

Working towards . . .

AUDIENCE
Will have some understanding of the concepts of focus, tension and release in relation to the audience's experience of drama. Will have an emerging understanding of the possible range of functions for theatre, including challenge, entertainment, education, celebration and ritual functions.

Working towards . . .

AUDIENCE
Will understand the active role of the audience in the making of meaning in drama and understand how meaning is made and remade through audience interaction. Will begin to be aware of concepts of empathy, catharsis and alienation and their importance in theatre. Will understand that dramas have a range of different functions for their audience across time and culture, and will be able to give specific examples.

Working towards . . .

CONTENT
Understands that drama is a means of communicating ideas and that it has a variety of functions and purposes. Is able to use simple drama forms that are suited to the communication of the student's own idea.

Working towards . . .

CONTENT
Has a developing understanding that good drama depends upon the successful integration of form and content. Is starting to experiment with different drama forms appropriate to the choice of content material.

Working towards . . .

CONTENT
Has a good understanding of the crucial relationship between form and content in drama. Understands that drama can be used to entertain, challenge, celebrate and persuade, and is able to demonstrate this through their own work. Can select content material that has dramatic potential across a wide range of forms and genres.

Conceptual knowledge and understanding assessment grid (student version)

Level 1	Level 2	Level 3
Working towards... **ROLE AND ACTING** When you act out a role, you are able to use your imagination to step into someone else's shoes for a while and imagine what it might be like to be a person in that situation.	*Working towards...* **ROLE AND ACTING** You are also able to build characters that are not just 'types' of person but are different from one another. You use your voice, face and body to show your character reacting to different situations.	*Working towards...* **ROLE AND ACTING** You understand that there is a wide range of different acting styles (for instance, stylised or movement-based work, or more naturalistic acting). You can choose the kind of acting that suits your work best.
Working towards... **FORM AND SYMBOL** When you are making drama with your teacher, you know the difference between realistic drama (*drama that tries to be like real life*) and stylised or abstract drama (*drama that might be exaggerated, symbolic or larger than life*). When you are given a story to turn into drama, you can create scenes that use images (*like still image or frozen pictures*) as well as words in an interesting way.	*Working towards...* **FORM AND SYMBOL** When you are working in groups, you are also able to include abstract or stylised elements like still image, slow motion and mime in your work in order to create different kinds of meaning. You understand that drama is made up of signs and symbols that represent ideas and feelings, actions, people or places. You know these symbols communicate meaning to the audience, and you deliberately use these to make your work better.	*Working towards...* **FORM AND SYMBOL** You are familiar with a wide range of drama styles (naturalistic, reportage, physical theatre, etc.), and can use elements of these to make original drama work of your own. You are skilled in using symbols and metaphors in your drama that capture the essence or meaning of the work effectively. You are able to place these successfully into your drama work.
Working towards... **STRUCTURE** When you plan and create your drama, they are straightforward plays that contain a beginning, middle and an end. With some help you can use conventions like flashback to change the way the plot unfolds.	*Working towards...* **STRUCTURE** When you plan and create your drama you often use techniques such as *flashback, flashforward* and *cross-cutting*. You understand that these different ways of structuring drama, create different effects for an audience.	*Working towards...* **STRUCTURE** Your work shows that you can use of a range of possible structures to create drama and you can give examples of similar structures found in existing plays and scripts, television, film or radio.
Working towards... **STAGE** When you are working on your drama, you have some understanding of how the use of space, props, music, sound and light can help to make the meaning of a drama clearer or more interesting.	*Working towards...* **STAGE** When given the opportunity, you use space effectively to show different relationships of characters and their different status. You can suggest ways of using light and sound to indicate ideas such as isolation or to create mood and atmosphere.	*Working towards...* **STAGE** You can visualise and then actually include design elements that add higher levels of meaning to your work. For example, a cage might be used as a metaphor to show a high school girl's isolation, coloured pools of light might reflect a character's journey over time, and a mask might show authority.
Working towards... **TEXT** You know that drama is not always written down and that an improvisation can be a kind of drama text. You understand that a playscript has lots of information for the performer and that it forms the basis for a performance. With help, you can use the script as a plan for your own performance.	*Working towards...* **TEXT** You are willing to try out and experiment with improvised and scripted drama texts. You understand that drama based on scripts and improvisations has *subtext* (hidden meanings found in the words, silences and actions of the characters). You know that these meanings can be acted out differently and they can make the drama mean different things.	*Working towards...* **TEXT** You can compose different kinds of drama texts by using a variety of methods. You are able to read and interpret a playscript and can use it to direct a group of other people. You can take into account stage directions (*instructions for the actor on how to say lines, when to move or what to do*), character interpretation (*how the actor might act as the character*), subtext and the playwright's intention.

continued

Student version continued

Level 1	Level 2	Level 3
AUDIENCE *Working towards...* When you plan, shape and perform your drama work, you know the audience is an essential part of the experience. You might make some decisions that take the audience into consideration.	**AUDIENCE** *Working towards...* As you create your drama, you often use different techniques like narration or direct address (*speaking directly to the audience*) to create different relationships between the performer and the audience. You are beginning to understand that an audience can be emotionally involved in the drama in different ways.	**AUDIENCE** *Working towards...* You are aware of a range of techniques and theatre forms that create specific audience/performer relationships. You can give examples of how this works in plays you have looked at and in your own drama. You take into account the effect of your drama techniques on the audience and deliberately intend them to be affected in different ways.
CONTENT *Working towards...* You are able to use realistic drama (*acting that tries to be like real life*) to express your own ideas. You are aware that drama is around us and part of our society and that it can be used for different purposes.	**CONTENT** *Working towards...* You are aware of a range of different drama forms and can select the best one to communicate your ideas to an audience. You know that sometimes drama challenges the audience to think about what it is watching and make a decision about the themes and issues in it.	**CONTENT** *Working towards...* You understand that good drama depends on form *and* content (*what is in the drama – the themes and ideas*) working well together and that some content might be suited to a very specific type of drama. You understand that drama can be used to entertain, celebrate and challenge and can give examples from your own work, plays you have looked at or the work of other people in your group.

Conceptual knowledge and understanding record sheet (for students)

NAME _____ FORM _____	Date (Example)	Date	Date	Date	Date
Role and acting – how you take on roles and portray characters in your drama.	*Level 1*				
Form and symbol – ideas about different types of drama and how they work; how you use images and ideas in your drama that may have a number of meanings.	*Working towards L1*				
Structure – choices you make about the way your drama works (how it may be broken into separate sections, how the story unfolds, how you deal with changes in time or place).	*Working towards L2*				
Stage – how you use the space, props, sound, music or light.	*Level 1*				
Text – how you use texts and scripts to create drama.	*Level 2*				
Audience – how you plan and perform your drama in order to have an effect on the audience.	*Level 3*				
Content – what your drama is about: the ideas, themes or issues it explores.	*Working towards L2*				

Group skills audit

Date _____	Name _____
Form _____	Teacher _____

We all contribute in different ways during group work. This table will help you identify the way you enjoy working.

- First, read all the descriptions carefully.
- Now divide 20 marks between the descriptions that you think sum up your style of working the best. You can choose as many or as few categories as you like.
- Alongside the category with the most marks, write an example of something you actually did during any of the tasks.

Provider
You provide the ideas for the rest of the group to work on. Often this is at the very beginning of the task. Sometimes you can provide lots of different ideas, or even ones that contrast with each other.

Here's my idea . . .
My thoughts are . . .
I think . . .

Solver
You solve problems when the work stalls or fails to move forward. This might mean encouraging the rest of the group to consider other ideas or approaches. Often your ideas are very different to the way the work has developed up to that point.

Why don't we . . .
How about . . .
What if we . . .

Profiler
You enjoy shaping the ideas of other people, often changing them to suit the drama. You enjoy listening to the rest of the group and joining in when you hear an idea that you think is good.

That's good, but why don't we . . .
I see, and then we could . . .
Instead of that, we could . . .

Builder
You help turn the group's ideas into concrete drama that can be performed or shared. Once the group has decided upon an idea, you are the one who encourages the group to get up and try the ideas out. You keep an eye on the time.

Right, let's get going . . .
Come on, we can make a start . . .
Let's move the chairs . . .

Leader
You have a clear idea of what the finished drama will look like. This might mean telling other people in the group what to do or say.

Why don't you?
Let's run through it again . . .
Try it from over here . . .

Watcher
You engage with the work, but tend to listen and watch as the group develops its ideas. You prefer to be told what to do, although you can make the work your own when you are clear about your role in the drama.

Should I . . .?
What can I do . . .?
What are we doing . . .?

Critic
You are able to evaluate the work as you rehearse or prepare and when you perform. Your comments and suggestions make the drama more effective.

It was good when . . .
When she did this it was . . .
The drama worked best when . . .

Negative blocker
You tend to stop the drama work by arguing or disagreeing with ideas and suggestions or criticising the work without suggesting good alternatives.

That's stupid . . .
I'm not doing that . . .
This isn't working . . .

Positive blocker
You encourage the work to move forward by stopping input from anyone in the group who is being negative or preventing progress.

Stop messing about . . .
Don't interrupt . . .
That's not helping . . .

Student self-assessment sheet

Student self-assessment sheet for   **unit** _____

Name _____

Form _____

Date _____

Understanding and knowledge

1 What *drama words* have you learnt during these activities? List them and say what they mean.

_____

_____

_____

_____

_____

2 Describe some of the *theatre techniques* you learnt about during this work. How have you used them?

_____

_____

_____

_____

_____

Topic specific evaluative question 1:

_____

_____

_____

_____

Topic specific evaluative question 2:

_____

_____

_____

_____

_____

Personal and social skills

To what extent did you:

- Contribute to group discussion or planning?

- Take part in problem-solving and decision making?

- Co-operate to plan and present drama?

- Negotiate with others in the group?

Can you provide examples?

Performance skills
Can you describe a moment in the drama when you – or others in your group – performed well? What made this a good performance?

_____

_____

_____

_____

_____

Response to the drama
Choose a character from the drama. Write a letter home, or a diary account, *in role as that person*. You might wish to discuss this task with your teacher.

_____

_____

_____

_____

_____

Reflective writing
Describe a moment in the drama that was particularly effective. Why did it work for you? You might wish to discuss this task with your teacher.

_____

_____

_____

_____

_____

continued

Self-assessment

Look at the 'Conceptual knowledge and understanding assessment grid' (student version). Your teacher will tell you which strand (row) of the grid to focus on for this unit. Reflecting on the work that you have done, find your level on the grid. In the box below write an example of something that you have done that is evidence for your choice.

Strand: _____

Level: _____

Evidence:

_____

_____

_____

_____

_____

_____

_____

_____

_____

_____

_____

Target setting

Using the grid, try to write a target – something you can do in future drama lessons – that will help move you towards the next level in the grid.

Current level in the grid: _____

Next level in the grid: _____

Your target:

_____

_____

_____

_____

_____

_____

_____

_____

Suggested specific evaluative questions for the units

Unit 1: Urban Legends

- Describe how you used *flashback* in your work.
- What is *physical theatre*? How did you use it in your work?

Unit 2: Dilemmas

- What is *subtext*? Can you give an example of a subtext in your own work?
- What did you learn about *stage* and *film/TV* drama in this project?

Unit 3: Displaced People

- Describe what *narration* means. Can you describe different ways of presenting narration? What affects do these different ways have on the audience?
- Describe some drama you have created that was based on *fact*. What problems did you face? How did you overcome them?

Unit 4: Next Stop . . . High School

- Describe how you used *stereotypes* and *stock characters* in your work.
- Is drama a good way of *teaching* things to people? Why not just 'tell them'?

Unit 5: Lilliput

- This drama works through the use of *analogy* – by creating a *parallel* situation, which at first seems strange but which is similar to real life in some ways. Can you think of other uses of this technique in TV, film or stage drama? Why do authors and playwrights use analogies, do you think?
- When constructing your *propaganda film*, what techniques did you use to show your own side in a good light, and the other side in a negative way?

Unit 6: The White Rose

- Describe what *dramatic tension* means. Can you describe different ways of creating dramatic tension? What effects do these different ways have on the audience?
- Describe some of the differences between *naturalistic* and more *stylised* theatre.

Unit 7: The Mysteries

- How did you use *ritual* in your work? Why was it effective?
- What did you learn about working from a *script* in this project?

Unit 8: The Toodyay Letters

- Describe some of the *problems* you encountered in dramatising and staging the Toodyay letters. How did you *overcome* them?
- Draw a 'map' of the *structure* of your Toodyay letters dramas. Which do you think was most effective? Why?

Part 2

The teaching units

Introduction to the teaching units

At the start of each unit there is an introduction that should help shape and build the context of the work for both the teacher and the class. The activities provide very detailed step-by-step guidance as to the delivery of the work. Again, we would like to point out that the tasks and instructions are not meant to be prescriptive. Our hope is that all teachers and facilitators exercise their right to take the work in directions that suit the needs and learning styles of their students, and such departures should be seen as part of the experience of the units. Some of the tasks will require photocopies of the resources found at the end of each unit.

As the units are comprehensive and fairly substantial in content and length, the brief 'map' of the activities might prove useful in recording the progress of the group. Likewise, using the evaluation sheets will encourage students' reflection and self-assessment, and some suggested unit-specific questions are provided.

Urban legends

Introduction and context

'This *really* happened to a friend of a friend of mine . . .' – the familiar opening of an urban legend. Urban legends or myths can be seen as the modern equivalent of more traditional folklore or fairy stories. The importance of folklore and the oral tradition as a means of communicating religious, moral or instructional tales and fables to a predominately illiterate population is well documented. What better way of warning children about the dangers of straying off the literal and symbolic path, than to tell them the tale of Little Red Riding Hood?

The processes of legend formation and transmission remain the same for modern urban legends as they did for traditional stories. Literacy and mass communication are at unparalleled levels, yet urban legends continue to serve – and some might say thrive – as apocryphal folk tales set in the recent past. Ironically, although myths and legends are often seen as belonging in our distant past, the urban legend is very firmly rooted in the present, and global communication revolutions such as television and the Internet have ensured their proliferation.

Although the content of urban legends differs, they share certain traits that help us identify them:

- The tales are told as 'true' stories and are often believed both by the teller and the audience listening.
- The legends often have local variations that make them more believable to the audience. These are specific details like location, setting, time or characters involved.
- The tales reflect the fears of modern society and they often have a cautionary, moral or instructional element.
- The audience will normally be familiar with many such tales, some of which have been told and retold for generations.
- The stories might have an unexplained or supernatural element to them.

During this project, the students will have the opportunity to investigate urban legends from a number of perspectives, as well as working practically to dramatise them and gain an insight into particular stories. However, rather than just use the stories as interesting stimuli for drama, the pupils will also be able to speculate as to:

- Origin: Where did the stories come from? Who told them for the first time and to whom?
- Function: What are the stories 'for'? Why do we tell them to each other?
- Meaning: What do the stories tell us about ourselves or our society?

The drama will explore theatrical skills and ideas related to narrative structure and storytelling, introducing the techniques of linear narrative, flashback and cross-cutting. The students will also have opportunities to experiment with physical theatre form.

We anticipate that a group exploring all the activities in this unit would take about four one-hour lessons to complete the tasks.

Urban legends **unit map**

Activity	Description	Resources	Teacher notes
Activity 1	Introduction to urban legends; sharing stories; *The Vanishing Hitch-hiker*.	Resource sheet 1	
Activity 2	*The Vanishing Hitch-hiker* dramatisation.		
Activity 3	Apply flashback structure to the story.		
Activity 4	Teacher in role, establishing time travel element; investigating origins of story. One group investigating *Spider in the Hairdo* story.	Resource sheet 2	
Activity 5	One group shares *Spider in Hairdo* story. Introduce medieval sermon – *Lady of Eyensham*.	Resource sheet 3	
Activity 6	Dramatising the medieval story; status games.	Resource sheet 3	
Activity 7	Dramatising the medieval story; the fourteenth-century church.	Resource sheet 3	
Activity 8	Bringing the spider to life: groups of five or six. Teacher in role as priest – cross-cut between 'church' and 'spider'	Resource sheet 3	
Activity 9	*Metamorphosis*: script parallel.	Resource sheet 4	

Activity I

Gather the pupils into a circle and tell them the story of *The Vanishing Hitch-hiker*. It is important that you emphasise that the events in the story are 'true'. The story will become even more believable if you add local detail or knowledge that roots the tale firmly in the present and in a specific location; the friends could be travelling back from a well-known landmark or particular event perhaps.

> *A friend of a friend was driving with his companion through a remote part of the country. It was a stormy night, with strong winds and torrential rain. On a bend in the road they were surprised to see in the beam of the car's headlights a young woman hitching a lift. She was not dressed for such poor weather, and was soaked to the skin and shivering. They decided to stop and pick her up. As the girl settled on the back seat she looked a bit dazed, and asked if they would take her to her home, about five miles along the road. As they drove, the girl indicated that they should pull off the road down a farm track.*
>
> *After following the track for some time, they eventually came to an old farmhouse and pulled up outside the front door. The two friends turned round to tell the girl they had arrived – and she had vanished! She was nowhere to be seen. The only logical explanation was that she had quickly opened the door, got out of the car and dashed into the farmhouse.*
>
> *They decided to check and see if she had got into the house safely, so they braved the rain and knocked on the front door. After a while, an elderly couple came to the door. The two friends explained about the girl they had tried to help on the road. As they told their story, a strange look came over the faces of the couple. They said that they did have a daughter, but that she had disappeared whilst coming home from a night out five years ago. Today would have been her birthday . . .*

Ask the students if any of them recognise the story. Do they know of other similar stories? You may wish to invite any volunteers to retell other urban legends of which they are aware, but avoid allowing the students to simply swap ghost stories. Urban legends have certain criteria that make them what they are. If necessary, retell some other 'key' urban legends you might know for the class to discuss (see Resource sheet 1, page 45). The pupils are often very enthusiastic about swapping these stories, and this process of telling the tales can get in the way of advancing the drama. You may wish to save more examples of the stories as a reward, once the first phase of the work has been done.

Introduce to the group the identifying factors of urban legends:

- Urban legends are usually orally transmitted – passed on by word of mouth.
- The stories are told as if they are true, unlike jokes or 'fairy stories'. Indeed, urban legends are often found presented as fact in newspaper reports.
- The teller often includes details of specific people, times or locations.
- The tales are often bizarre or surprising, or have elements of horror. Many of them have learning or moral content.
- They rarely claim to have happened to the narrator directly, but usually to a relative or a 'friend of a friend'.
- Similar stories or 'variants' have been told for generations. Versions of stories like *The Vanishing Hitch-hiker*, first recorded in the United States in the 1960s, continue to be told today.
- New urban legends are being created continuously, and the Internet is a very fruitful resource for the latest stories. As well as being instrumental in circulating urban legends, the Internet is itself the subject of hundreds of stories.

Activity 2

Explain to the group that in order to find out more about the story of *The Vanishing Hitch-hiker*, they are going to use it as the basis of a piece of drama.

In groups of three or four, ask the students to decide on the key moments of the story. If you think your students need reminding, read out the text again. However, there is something interesting to be explored in the way the students decide to re-tell their version of the story after hearing it only once. Does the group embellish the facts or introduce new characters or dialogue? What does this tell us about the nature of urban legends and storytelling in general?

Once they have selected their key moments, ask the groups to use these as a basis for five or six still images that communicate their version of the story effectively. Instruct the groups to link their tableaux sequences by speaking parts of the original story as narration. (See Unit 3, page 70, for a comprehensive table of narrative forms.)

Allow the groups to work for a few minutes, then stop the students and ask them to refine their improvisations to include:

- enough details of gesture and facial expressions to make the characters and relationships clear to an audience;
- compositional elements such as the use of levels and space;
- the placing of the narrator with relation to the actors on stage and the audience watching. The students may wish to share the narrator role with characters stepping out of the action and delivering their lines;
- any design elements such as lighting or sound that enhance the drama.

Ask them also to consider:

- a sense of place – where is the story set?
- a sense of time – when does the story take place?
- a sense of mood and atmosphere – how do they want the audience to feel as they listen to the story?

Once the sequences have been refined, ask each group to present their work. During the evaluation, ask the class to identify similarities or differences between the ways the group approached the task and whether there were any significant differences between their versions.

Explain that you will now be looking at how the character of the hitch-hiker was represented by the different actors in their groups. In each group, identify the student who had represented the character of the hitch-hiker. In the centre of the circle, ask them to recreate their pose as they waited by the side of the road. Freeze all the hitch-hikers for 30 seconds and ask the audience to describe what they see. On the board, write down the adjectives used to describe the various portrayals, and note any commonalities or contrasting features.

Ask the class to reflect upon the representations. Does the way the girl is represented affect the meaning of the story? For instance, do we think differently about the story if the girl is portrayed as alternatively weak, desperate or assertive?

One feature of the story is that the hitch-hiker never reaches 'home'. In the supernatural world of the story, she continues to haunt the roadside. In the next task students will use flashback techniques to create dramatic explorations based on this question:

Why is the hitch-hiker's spirit so restless and why does she never reach home?

Activity 3

Ask the group to define the term 'flashback'. They may have they seen examples of this technique in films, television and theatre. Can they identify devices or techniques used to signal flashback?

One method of signalling flashback is by narration or voiceover and while this is entirely appropriate and effective, there are more sophisticated ways. Film and television use visual techniques such as cross-fades or dissolves, and theatre lighting can be used in a similar way. Music can be used as an indicator of a particular era, or a time change can be signalled by a sound motif. The students might want to experiment by using sounds, words, chants or gestures to indicate the flashback, for example by repeating a phrase of the dialogue (. . . *today would have been her birthday* . . .). It could be that the scene in flashback is presented in a different style from scenes depicted in 'the present'.

Discuss how the use of flashback and the manipulation of time in a drama can create a specific effect for the audience. Audiences aware of the ultimate outcome of a drama will engage with the action from a position of knowledge or foresight. This different perspective will influence the way in which dramatic tension is built and maintained. Furthermore, as the audience already knows the ending, they are less concerned with what will happen and more focused upon the 'why' and 'how' of the action.

Give the students the following structure from which to work:

- Scene 1: The parents' house. *Yes we had a daughter, but she disappeared five years ago . . .*
- Scene 2: The flashback sequence. This is an explanation of what happened to the girl and the reason she never made it back home on that fateful night.
- Scene 3: The roadside. *Look, a hitch-hiker . . . let's pick her up . . .*

Working in the same groups from the last task, ask the students to create a sequence of three scenes. The work is to progress from tableau to include movement and dialogue, but scenes one and three should start with the still image devised previously. The students will have to consider what they think actually happened to the girl on that night. Encourage the groups to come up with as many imaginative ideas as possible, reminding them that the implication of violence is more sinister than attempting to portray it naturalistically.

The other element of the work is to ask the students to find a technique that signals their flashback sequence clearly. Remind them of the methods discussed earlier, and again encourage them to think beyond the obvious narration (*Five years ago . . .*). Once the scenes are devised and presented, conduct a focused evaluation using the following questions:

- *Which drama was most effective and why?*
- *How did each group provide an answer to the key question of what happened to the girl?*
- *Why is flashback a useful technique?*
- *What do we now feel about the story?*
- *Why do you think people continue to tell this story and why are stories like this popular?*

Activity 4

In this section students will use drama to investigate the possible origin of the story. Either write a notice on the board or use Resource sheet 2 (page 46) to indicate the setting of the next phase of the drama. The notice on the board might read:

TimeSlip Investigations

'Witness the past and change the future.'

Mission Project 1:

Urban legends and their origins – *The Vanishing Hitch-hiker.*

TimeSlip Investigations welcomes its team of expert investigators and researchers.

Ask the group to set out chairs for a meeting in a conference hall. Explain that in this phase of the work, they will have to take on the 'expert' role of investigators and researchers who work for TimeSlip Investigations. As the name suggests, this is no ordinary group of private investigators. TimeSlip has unique access to a time machine and uses it to send their investigators back in time to witness specific events first hand. Explain that you will be taking on the role of chief executive of TimeSlip Investigations.

In role, welcome the 'investigators' to the conference:

> *Welcome to this, the first of a series of mission meetings for the latest commission for TimeSlip Investigations. As you know, we use our unique ability to send investigators back in time to witness real events, as they happened in the past. The latest investigation we have been hired to carry out is for a very highly regarded university. They are exploring the origins of urban legends and modern folklore and are trying to identify the exact moment when one of these stories was first told. I'm sure you are all familiar with the urban legend known as* The Vanishing Hitch-hiker?
>
> *The university concerned wants us to specifically find out:*
>
> - *Who first told the story?*
> - *Who did they tell it to?*
> - *Why did they tell it?*
>
> *I know you are all familiar with the story, but in order to help us program the TimeSlip machine accurately, does anyone have any theories as to who might have told the story for the first time, and why did they tell it?*

Encourage the students to present as many different theories as possible. Was it a parent attempting to warn their children about the dangers of walking home late at night? Was it a landowner trying to warn children off or away from his land? Was it an enterprising businesswoman trying to invent a local legend for tourism purposes? Was it a writer or author trying out a story with an audience? Was it a misheard or misunderstood news item on the radio or in a newspaper article?

Finish the meeting by explaining that, working in small groups, they will be able to choose where and when in time they want to return to for their investigation. In these groups of three or four, ask the students to devise a short piece of drama that recreates what they saw when they went back in time and remind them that they are not re-telling the story, they are showing the precise moment when they think the urban legend was first told. The students should:

- be clear about when and where the drama is set;
- consider the characters involved by demonstrating clearly who is telling the story and whom they are telling it to;
- consider why the storyteller is telling the story – what is their motivation?

Each drama should last a maximum of one minute, but before working practically the groups must answer the three focusing questions. Providing them with a piece of sugar paper and a pen will allow them to write down their responses. Again, it is important to stress to the pupils that they are not simply re-enacting the story but are investigating the first time the story was told to someone else. They can change some things from the original – such as the mode of transport – to suit different times or cultures if necessary, but the gist of the story should remain intact.

Allow the groups a short devising period. At this point, discreetly select a group who will accept a separate mission. Explain that as the time machine begins to work, their group is diverted somewhat and they end up exploring a different story. Read them *The Spider in the Hairdo* story.

The Spider in the Hairdo

A friend of a friend knew someone back in the 1960s who worked in a hairdressing salon. It was a time when lots of young women used to back-comb their hair, teasing it into a pile on to the top of their heads in a variety of flamboyant styles, the most popular being called 'the Beehive'. To create these hair sculptures, people used to use lots of lacquer and spray to get their hair to stay up . . . and that meant not washing their hair for weeks.

A young woman went to this particular hairdressers to get her hair restyled. The hairdresser started to snip at the almost rock solid hair and the woman immediately started to complain of stabbing pains in her scalp.

The alarmed hairdresser then parted the hair and found the woman's head swarming with tiny poisonous tarantula spiders. What had happened was that an adult spider had made a nest in the poor teenager's lacquered hair. Disturbed by the movement of the scissors, the spiders bit her scalp and she died a painful death.

Ask the group to identify five key moments from the story and use these moments as the basis for five still images. Explain that this will be their contribution to the feedback when the other groups share their *Vanishing Hitch-hiker* work. Explain also that they should keep their separate mission a secret from the rest of the investigators.

Before the students present their work, remind the group that their task was to go back in time and bring back research for experts on folklore. Adopt the role of the chief executive again and ask each group to present their work 'to the conference', leaving the 'spider' group until last.

After the students have performed their dramas, explain that the group has now witnessed a number of possible 'theories' related to the origins of *The Vanishing Hitch-hiker* story. They must now choose the version they think the experts on folklore would consider the most likely to have occurred. Encourage the students to justify their choices and be aware that, paradoxically, the most effective drama may not necessarily be the most convincing or likely theory of the story's origin.

- *Does this work help us to understand how urban legends may have started?*
- *Do we have any ideas about why urban legends are told?*
- *To whom are urban legends normally directed?*
- *What is this particular story's 'message' and do we agree with it?*
- *Why are the 'victims' of many of these stories young women?*

Activity 5

The students will probably have noticed that one of the groups did not share their work. If necessary return to your role of chief executive of TimeSlip to explain:

> *As you know, the science of time-travel is not exact and one group was diverted from the Vanishing Hitch-hiker task, but interestingly found another urban legend that may be of interest to our clients. Unfortunately the recording device they used to capture the story became corrupted during their return journey back to present day. As a result, we have a series of images for you to look at. Can you decipher what the story is about?*

Allow the 'spider' group to share their images and encourage the students in role as investigators to present their theories as to what the story is about, who it is happening to and when it is set. If necessary, finish by re-telling the story to the whole group.

In the light of their findings from the previous activity, it may be interesting to note that this story also seems to fit the pattern of modern-day morality tales aimed specifically at young women.

Ask the students if they can identify any 'moral' that might be present in this story. The students may be able to identify moral imperatives in relation to issues of cleanliness, excess or vanity. It is interesting to note that, at the time, flamboyant hairstyles of this kind were popular amongst a newly recognised social group causing controversy by their lack of moral standards, namely, *teenagers*.

Returning to the role as chief executive, introduce the next piece of evidence:

> *As well as this modern spider urban legend, the time machine also presented another piece of very interesting evidence. Like the last example, this has been corrupted somewhat, but we still have the audio track to listen to . . . it seems to date back 600 years – to the fourteenth century . . .*

If you have recorded the sermon on Resource sheet 3 (page 47), play it to the group now. Alternatively, simply read out the extract as a transcript.

After the group has heard the sermon, ask them to consider the age and possible context of the 'story'. Are there any similarities with the previous tale, especially regarding morals or homilies?

In his book *The Vanishing Hitch-hiker*, Jan Harold Brunvand refers to a sermon collected in a medieval chronicle that appears to have some similarities with urban legends like *The Spider in the Hairdo*. In the sermon, a lady of the village of Eynesham in Oxfordshire is punished for her vanity in spending too long 'over the adornment of her hair' and too little time in church. The devil descends upon her in the shape of a huge spider and attaches itself to her head. In spite of her protestations, the spider will not go until the abbot of the local abbey 'displayed the holy sacrament before it' (Brunvand, 1981: 78).

Activity 6

Explain to the class that, using the sermon as a starting point, they are going to recreate the setting, mood and atmosphere in order to re-enact the original church service with the congregation present:

- Where might the sermon have taken place?
- What might the church have looked like?
- Who might have been present?

To help them recreate the scene they will use techniques of simultaneous staging and cross-cutting, with an emphasis on physical theatre. To establish the context of a village church in the distant past, younger or less experienced groups may find the following exercises on status helpful.

First, introduce the following game, popularised by theatre director Max Stafford-Clark and often used as a rehearsal tool.

Ask the students to find a space in the room and give each of them a playing card face down. Once all the cards have been given out, explain that their card delineates their status and that the higher the value of the card, the higher their status. The king is the highest card of all and aces are the lowest.

Now instruct the students to look at their card, but not to show anyone else. Ask them to put their card in a pocket or safe place and to sit or stand in a manner that befits their new status. Quickly go round the group commenting on their poses and facial expressions. Next, ask them to move around the space and encounter as many people in the room as possible, attempting to communicate their status to others through the subtle use of greetings, eye contact and body language. After a few minutes, freeze the group and ask them to form a line from high to low status, carefully checking with others near to them that they have the correct place in the line.

Ask each student to reveal their card and discuss whether they were able to find their correct place in the line.

- *What does this tell us about how we recognise and communicate status?*
- *What 'cues' or gestures do we use as we speak to people?*
- *Do the phrases 'looking down your nose' or 'looking up to someone' offer clues about physicality and status?*

As a variation on this exercise, give each student a different card, but this time instruct them that they should not look at their card, but instead hold it, facing outwards, to their forehead. The game continues as before, but this time the task is for the students to ascertain their own status from the way that others behave towards them.

(For a detailed description of how these and other status games were used by Clark in his rehearsals of Farquhar's *The Recruiting Officer* see Clark, 1989).

Activity 7

Explain that in the next phase of the work the students will begin the process of recreating the fourteenth century church, and that this will require the students to take on a role.

We are going to become villagers in a small village church in England, some time in the fourteenth century.

Ask the class to consider who might live in such a village. List the student's ideas as to how the parishioners of the village might have earned a living:

- *Did everyone work?*
- *What crafts or skills might people have?*
- *Are some skills more highly prized than others?*
- *What differences between rich and poor might be apparent?*
- *Could people read and write, and if they couldn't how would they get information or news?*
- *Who is in authority in the village?*

Introduce the idea that the village consists of a mainly illiterate population made up of labourers having to work on land they rented and did not own. The power lies with the clergy, and with a few rich families who possess the majority of the wealth and the land. There are also artisans who support themselves and their families by providing services or making things that others need. Highlight the importance of the church and religion as a stabilising factor in an uncertain world. For the people of the time many of the seemingly incomprehensible things in life, such as the spread of disease, the cycle of the seasons or even the sun setting and rising, had their explanation in the pages of the Bible. Because so few people could read, the church was the place where most people received their moral and religious instruction. With the pupils' help, define the space to resemble a church by placing chairs in rows, facing a pulpit represented by a desk, stage block or lectern. Instruct the group to enter the 'church' and sit down on one of the 'pews'. Once seated, explain that their distance from the pulpit defines their status in the village – the further to the rear of the church they sat, the lower their status, power and influence. (Alternatively, the class may wish to refer back to the playing card exercise and use their random cards to dictate their status.)

Once the students are settled 'in the church', ask each of them to select a role and occupation that corresponds with their defined status.

In role as the priest, welcome the congregation to the church, especially thanking them for their prompt attendance. Once all are assembled, begin the story of the woman who was late, telling it as the sermon for the day with a suitably stern delivery, using Resource sheet 3.

Alternatively, you may wish to dramatise the giving of the sermon more symbolically by playing the original tape of the sermon whilst the group holds a tableau.

At the end of the sermon, thought track a few individuals by asking them to respond in role to the following questions:

- Who do they think the priest is referring to?
- Have they ever been late to church?
- Do they believe the story?

Activity 8

Once there is a range of responses from the congregation, stop the drama and introduce the next phase of the work. Explain that the group is going to use the techniques of physical theatre to recreate the horrific images that the villagers might imagine as they listen to the spider sermon.

You may need to explain how physical theatre differs from more naturalistic forms. In this kind of theatre, emphasis is placed on the use of the actor's own resources – body and voice – to physicalise the text in highly stylised ways. Very often physical theatre performances have minimal set, costume or props – the focus of the audience is upon the performer. In this way movement, language and gesture take on a heightened significance. In this highly abstract form, the audience has to become imaginatively engaged in order to decode and interpret what is happening on stage.

The writer, actor and director Stephen Berkoff is an eminent practitioner of this style of theatre:

> I believe that you don't need anything more than just utter simplicity and that everything in my art must be created from the body onwards. The body and the voice. Everything else is an imposition and is an interference with the art of the actor: if it's too many lights, too many props. So the simplicity with me is that I return the art of the actor to the actor; not give it to the sets or give it to the props or give it to the costumes or give it to the lights. But give it to the performer.
>
> (Berkoff, 1990)

The benefits of this approach to acting are that it allows the performers the freedom to represent anything on stage. Stephen Berkoff insists that there is nothing that cannot be represented by an actor and their body. His actors work as an ensemble to create highly stylised characters, as well as the physical environments they inhabit and the objects they handle. For actors, the challenge of this approach comes from the emphasis upon individual and disciplined technical movement and mime skills that often require a high degree of physical prowess, strength and stamina.

In groups of five or six, set the students the task of bringing the spider to life using physical theatre techniques. The groups must consider how they will represent the spider by capturing the essence of the movement of the creature and its sense of menace. The spider should be an ensemble creation involving all of the group as well as being animated so that it can swoop on the unfortunate woman! Ask the students to consider the scuttling motion of a spider. How can they represent this movement? Is it possible to divide up the image into legs, body or mandibles? How could they incorporate sounds to make their creation more alarming?

Once the groups have established a way of presenting the spider, they will need to divide their drama into distinct parts that correspond with the story. Give the groups Resource sheet 3 broken into four sections that detail the sermon. They can select particular parts of the text to cue the movement of the spider and the victim's reaction.

After a sufficient amount of preparation time, ask the groups to present their spiders in turn. As a whole group, decide which is the most dramatic, and identify why it is the most effective.

Ask one group to present their spider as if it is what the parishioners are imagining while the priest is delivering the sermon. Place this group on one side of the space, whilst the remainder of the class represents the congregation in the church. In role as the priest, begin retelling the sermon and, at appropriate moments, 'cross-cut' from one location to the other. As the spider descends on the woman freeze the action, come out of role, and thought-track some of the congregation:

- Are they frightened by the appearance of the devil in the form of a spider?
- Why has the woman been attacked?
- Are they always on time to church?
- Are they vain like the woman?
- Have they ever heard of anything like this before?
- As they see the spider in their imagination, what do they think?
- Do they know the priest; is he or she trying to frighten them?
- What about the other people in the church? Are there people in there to whom this story applies?

Evaluate the work by focusing upon the context of the story:

- *How does this tale compare with modern urban legends?*
- *Who is the story 'aimed at'?*
- *Is it an effective way of seeking to influence the people in the village? Do you think people would have been late to church again after hearing – and believing – this tale?*

Consider the theatre element:

- *Was physical theatre an effective way of presenting the spider?*
- *Are there any design elements that could support the drama or make the image clearer?*
- *Would this go against the nature of physical theatre and the emphasis upon the actor or actors to imaginatively portray the scene?*

Activity 9

As an extension to the work, you may wish to use the extract from Stephen Berkoff's *Metamorphosis* (Resource sheet 4, page 48), inspired from the novel of the same name by Franz Kafka, as an example of how a playwright uses physical theatre to present an insect on stage. After handing out the extract, explain that at the beginning of the play we see a 'flash-forward' – a premonition of what is going to happen to Gregor Samsa, the main character. He awakes one morning to find he has changed into a giant beetle. Although he can still think as a human being, he is trapped in an insect's body, unable to communicate with his family, for whom he is the main provider. Gregor has turned into what he feels about himself – a struggling insect – and the play explores how he and his family come to terms with their redefined roles following his transformation.

URBAN LEGENDS

Resource sheet I

The Lucky Businessman

A businessman was travelling in a remote part of the county by car. Desperate to find a toilet, he stopped at the first building he came across – a funeral home. Inside there were no people, but an open casket was laid out for viewing. Surprised at the lack of mourners at the funeral, the man respectfully said a prayer over the coffin and signed the guest book.

A few weeks later, the man received a call from a firm of lawyers. He was the sole beneficiary of a small fortune left by an old man who had passed away after secretly hiding his money for years. It seems that in the old man's will he had specified anyone who attended his funeral would have a share in his estate. The businessman was the only person who had signed the guest book and so he received everything.

The Hook

A young couple were kissing and cuddling in a car in a deserted country lane. A report came on the radio about the escape of a murderer from the local high security prison. The announcement emphasised that the prisoner should not be approached as he was considered to be highly dangerous. He could be identified by the metal hook he had instead of a right hand. On hearing this, the girl became anxious and wanted to go home. The boy became concerned too, started the engine and quickly sped off. When they reached the girl's house, the boy politely walked round the back of the car to let the girl out. As he reached down to open her door, he froze in surprise because there, hanging from the car's door handle, was a metal hook.

The Jealous Husband

A cement truck driver turned up unexpectedly at home one lunchtime and was surprise to see a brand new open-top sports car in his drive. Walking to the back door he saw his wife talking in a very animated fashion with a man in the kitchen. Suspecting his wife, the jealous husband returned to his truck, backed it up to the expensive car and delivered three tons of quick setting concrete through its open top. He then drove away. Returning home that night, his wife met him in tears . . . she had been secretly saving for years, his birthday present delivered that day had been destroyed . . . it was what he had always wanted . . . an open top sports car . . .

The Mouse in the Bottle

A couple were eating in a meal in a café. They ordered a well-know fizzy drink to go with their food. When the drinks arrived, they both took a deep swig straight from the bottle. The woman's drink tasted a little funny, so she drank some more to check. She then passed it to her partner to taste. He handed it back saying that it did indeed taste a bit strange. The woman took one last swig and, as the bottle tipped up, she was horrified to see half a dead mouse floating in the almost finished bottle.

Alligators In The Sewers

It so happens that some time ago a famous high street department store was selling baby alligators as a gimmick. These soon became the latest craze. Some months later, the alligators had grown considerably and many had become unsuitable for pets. Lots of these creatures were killed, but some were simply flushed down the toilet. The adolescent alligators thrived in the sewers, eating rats and goodness knows what else. It is said that the descendants of these first sewer alligators still inhabit the underground waterways, but now they are blind and have no colour to their skin due to the pitch black conditions.

TimeSlip Investigations

'Witness the past and change the future.'

Mission Project 1:

Urban legends and their origins – *The Vanishing Hitch-hiker.*

TimeSlip Investigations welcomes its team

of expert investigators and researchers.

URBAN LEGENDS

Resource sheet 3

Amongst our congregation, I'm afraid to say, there are those who are not as devout as they should be. As a timely reminder regarding the need to be punctual and conscientious in your attendance at church, remember the tale of the vain lady of Eynesham.

1   Famed as she was for her beauty, she would sit gazing at her own reflection and adorning her hair whilst others around her hurried to complete their labours and attend mass.

2   For many weeks her poor punctuality was noted, as were her attempts to creep unnoticed into the back of the church.

3   One day, without warning, a demon in the shape of a dreadful spider came down and wrapped its loathsome form about her head, gripping hard with hideous, twisted legs.

4   No matter how much she screamed and struggled, the spider would not let her be, but increased its grip until the lady feared for her very life.

5   Every possible remedy was administered, but the spider would not release the woman until the abbot presented the holy sacrament before it.

Think well on this sorry tale and learn.

URBAN LEGENDS

Resource sheet 4

Opening extract from *Metamorphosis* by Stephen Berkoff

The FAMILY enters one at a time – backcloth lit – figures appear in silhouette. Each one enters in the character he or she is going to play, and performs a small mime condensing the personality into a few seconds. MOTHER is first – describes a sad face – leaves a pained heart and angst. FATHER next strolls boldly on in boots and costume of mid-European lower middle-class tradesman – trousers in socks – braces – no jacket, looking like Hindenberg. Then GRETA, as student with violin. Then GREGOR, who just walks on and smiles – an amiable being.

As each speaks they form a line behind each other. On the last line they take on the movement of an insect by moving their arms to a particular rhythm. As no front lighting is used, this has the effect of an insect's leg movements.

MR S: [*enters*] As Gregor Samsa awoke one morning from uneasy dreams . . .
MRS S: [*enters*] He found himself transformed in his bed into a gigantic insect . . .
GRETA: [*enters*] His numerous legs, which were pitifully thin compared to the rest of his bulk, waved helplessly before him.

[*Movement starts. GREGOR is in front. Suddenly the movement stops – FAMILY dissolve the beetle image by moving away – leaving GREGOR still moving as part of the insect image.*]

[*Front lights come up revealing FAMILY.*]

GREGOR: What has happened to me?
FAMILY: He thought.
GREGOR: It was no dream.
GRETA: [*as clock*] He looked at the alarm clock ticking on the chest.
GREGOR: Half past six and the hands were quietly moving on.
MRS S: Gregor, Gregor?
MR S: Said a voice.
GREGOR: That gentle voice . . .
GRETA: It was his mother's . . .
MR S: His mother's . . .
MRS S: His mother's . . .

[*Fade.*]

Unit 2

Dilemmas

Introduction and context

The content of these short drama projects provides a context in which students can examine and clarify their own values towards a range of societal issues. Through carefully structured tasks, students are confronted with a dilemma or moral problem, and are then invited to explore different aspects of that problem in dramatic form. On one level, therefore, the work is 'process oriented' and learning objectives are broadly personal and social, and relate to the National Curriculum for Citizenship and Personal Social and Health Education (PSHE).

In addition to exploring a moral problem, however, students are also assisted in recording their work in the form of a written script. In this way explicit teaching about the notation, editing and structuring of scripts for the theatre stage and television studio is combined with the exploration of engaging and relevant social themes and issues. The 'product' so created can then be used as a basis for reflection on the themes and issues raised in the dramas, or might serve as a platform for more formal performance work. In following the unit, students will experience some of the difficulties faced by the playwright in creating scripts for others to interpret. They will also investigate the notion of *subtext*, and focus upon how subtextual elements are conveyed in dramatic action, and in scripted drama.

As in much work of this kind, teachers will need to be sensitive to the issues being explored and to the different life experiences students bring to their work. Through improvisation, the students are encouraged to analyse different perspectives and investigate the likely consequences of the fictional characters' actions. Judgements about how best to provide a supportive learning environment for students are heightened in this context: reminding the students of the pastoral resources in the school, and how they can use them, should always be built into reflection and evaluation time during each session.

We anticipate that a group exploring all the activities in this unit would take about seven one-hour lessons to complete the tasks.

Dilemmas **unit map**

Activity	Description	Resources	Teacher notes
Activity A1	Read newspaper story; teacher in role as eyewitness; hotseating.	Resource sheet 1	
Activity A2	Record memorable or effective phrases.		
Activity A3	Groups of four: role play – hospital waiting room.		
Activity A4	Record key phrases; add extra lines to form script; swap and perform.	Resource sheet 2	
Activity A5	Forum theatre: groups of four in the car at the moment of impact.		
Activity A6	Recording the dramatic sequence in A5.		
Activity A7	Role play: the passengers in the car at the bus stop.		
Activity A8	Record the role play in A7.		
Activity A9	Consequences . . .		
Activity A10	Recording the work in A9.		

Dilemmas unit map (continued)

Activity	Description	Resources	Teacher notes
Activity A11	*Reconciliation* dramas.		
Activity A12	Recording, drafting, redrafting; swap scripts and perform.		
Activity B1	Introduction; role play in threes: on the bus – finding the envelope.		
Activity B2	Recording the work: story boards; screenplay for first scene.		
Activity B4	Recording the work: story boards and minimal dialogue.		
Activity B5	Outside the big house: students plan their response.		
Activity B6	Recording the work: visual images without dialogue?		
Activity B7	Teacher in role – outside the big house: character chosen according to students' choices in B5.		
Activity B8	Recording the work: alternative endings to the drama.		

SECTION A: *HIT AND RUN* – SCRIPTING FOR THE STAGE

Activity A1

With the students in a circle, read out the newspaper article on Resource sheet 1 (page 62). Through careful questioning, aim to build up interest in the drama and encourage empathy for those involved:

- *What might have happened?*
- *Why did the driver not stop?*
- *How do you think the driver might feel now? How do you think the family of the victim might feel about what has happened?*

Working in role

By adopting the role of the eyewitness described in the newspaper account, the teacher can provide the group with an opportunity to question the witness about the accident. Other possible roles that may provide different perspectives on the incident – such as the police, or the paramedics attending the scene of the accident, could also be adopted. Care should be taken whilst working in role with the class in this way: it is imperative that the students are alerted to some of the dramatic possibilities of the situation, but not given too much information at this stage. The teacher will also have to make a number of decisions relating to the portrayal of the witness, and also to the *style* of the portrayal. These decisions will clearly depend upon the teacher's understanding of the function of this episode within the drama, and the intended learning outcomes.

- How much did the witness see?
- Is it more dramatic for the witness to have poor eyesight?
- How much can he or she remember?
- Is the drama more engaging or tense if the witness can't remember an important detail?
- How far should the character reveal personal feelings or prejudice about young people, or the justice system?
- How might the class's understanding of the situation be affected if, for instance, the witness is in favour of punitive custodial sentences for all offenders?
- How far should contextual detail – the witness's occupation; the type of neighbourhood; the music playing in the car, be revealed to the class?
- Will the class feel differently about the situation as a result?
- How far should the teacher *act?*

Accepted wisdom about teachers working in role with their class has tended to see 'role play' and 'acting' as distinct and separate:

> The key to effective taking on of . . . roles is *not acting* but simply taking a particular attitude that will promote thinking and responses from the children aimed towards a specific learning intention.
>
> (Toye and Prendiville, 2000: 20; our emphasis)

Role play, it is suggested, is *different* from acting in that the role player does not 'characterise', presenting only those physical and vocal signs that are absolutely necessary for the role to function in the drama (the 'role signifier'). According to this model the role player *remains him or herself* but in a fictionalised context. There may, of course, be very good educational reasons why modelling such economy – or lack of exaggerated theatricality – may be helpful in work of this kind, particularly when working with young children or with groups for whom the term 'acting' might serve as a de-motivator. However, it is clear that role playing is *acting* – albeit acting of a very particular kind.

In this drama it may be fruitful to experiment with the *playing* of the witness to the accident. This could range from a minimal portrayal where the function of the role in terms of *exposition* at the start of a drama is the main concern of the teacher, to a clear characterisation in which the teacher does much more than 'be themselves', providing a wealth of contextual detail, and a more consciously theatrical style of acting – and interacting – with the pupils. In our experience the key to fruitful interaction when working in role with pupils is careful questioning aimed at deepening the students' response – and this is not necessarily related to the acting style adopted by the teacher.

Activity A2: Recording the work

Once this section of the work is complete, ask each student to record any memorable or particularly effective phrases arising from the initial work in role. This material should be filed carefully as it will not be used until later stages of the project.

NOTE: As students will be working in the same group throughout this unit, it is important that each group keeps a file with copies of all scenes that are recorded: some will be the result of group efforts, and some the will be the result of solo tasks. In the latter case there will therefore be a number of possible versions filed. The final section of the unit will ask students to edit and select the material they have accumulated.

Activity A3

Form the students into groups of four and ask them to label themselves A, B, C and D in their groups:

- Who are we?   Tony's family and his doctor.
- Where are we?   A small, private waiting room.
- When are we?   Two days after the accident.

  A, B and C: I would like you to take on the roles of Tony's family. Decide amongst yourselves exactly who that might be – Tony's father, mother, brother or sister perhaps. You are at the hospital and it is almost two days since the accident. Tony is still in a coma. The doctor looking after him has asked to speak to you. You are in a small private waiting room.

Bring together the other members of the group (D) and brief them separately:

  You are to take on the role of the doctor who has been caring for Tony. It appears that Tony is coming out of his coma. An hour ago he spoke to the nurses looking after him. Apart from his broken arm and ribs, it looks as if he will make a full recovery.

Using parallel play (in which all the students work simultaneously but separately in their own space) allow the family members to establish the space and their roles, before the doctor joins the drama. Allow each group to improvise their reactions to the news. If appropriate, share some of the work.

Activity A4: Recording the work

Ask each group to record key sentences and phrases spoken by the characters in this improvisation on separate pieces of paper. Once recorded, ask the groups to assemble the phrases in an order which 'makes sense' in terms of the scene:

Read the 'script' so far. What else is needed to give a picture of what really took place in the improvisation? Write extra lines for each character to flesh out the scene. These may or may not have been actually spoken within the drama.

Once the groups have had a chance to script the extra lines required, ask them to record the whole scene on paper – up to 20 lines of dialogue – in the agreed order. For students who need support in this activity consult Resource sheet 2 (page 63), which provides an example of traditional stage play notation.

- *As a group, try to perform your scene from the script you have written. How does it differ from the improvised version? What further additions are needed?*
- *What stage directions might be added to allow a reader from another group to make sense of the script? Write any stage directions and be sure to make it clear that these are different from the lines of dialogue – by using a different colour – or putting them inside brackets, etc.*

As an extension activity, ask groups to swap finished scripts, and to compare their treatment of the scene with others. Do the scenes work as drama?

Make sure that the groups file the finished scenes (groups may prefer to word-process them) as 'The Hospital'.

Activity A5

Organise the group into a circle with a large enough performance space in the middle for the following action:

We are going to use the technique of 'forum theatre' to explore this drama further. In this kind of work you can control the drama as it is being acted out. If you want to change one of the actor's lines, or the way they are representing the character, you must say 'stop', and be prepared to make your suggestion, or even stand up and replace someone in the drama. The actors must carry on until someone stops them and changes something. We need someone to play the role of Barry, who is the driver who caused the accident, and three others to be his friends in the car. If we were going to create a still image of Barry and his friends immediately after the accident when the car is stationary, what would it look like?

(The gender and names of the characters in the drama can, of course, be changed to suit the group.)

Once the group is happy with the image, allow the students to improvise their reactions to the accident by 'bringing the image to life'.

- *Does anyone in the audience think they may have reacted differently?*
- *Do you think they may have said different things, been more shocked, or perhaps more eager to get away?*

As group members make suggestions, encourage them to take their place in the improvisation and allow it to run through a number of times, comparing and contrasting the various versions.

Activity A6: Recording the work

Ask the group for ideas of how versions of this scene might be recorded in written form:

- *What is important about 'the essence' of this scene? Of all the versions explored, which was most theatrically effective? Why?*

Ask each group to write a description of the dramatic sequence that makes up the chosen scene. It is important that actors who have taken no part in the original improvisation can follow these written descriptions. Although it is likely that the sequence will contain some dialogue, very effective dramatic sequences may consist of unconnected expletives, actors talking over each other, or indeed long periods of silence. How might these effects be recorded?

Ensure that the students file their finished 'scenes' as 'Car Scene' in their group's file.

Activity A7

- Who are we?   Friends of the driver who caused the accident.
- Where are we?   At the bus stop.
- When are we?   The morning after the accident.

Working in the same groups of four or five:

It is Monday morning after the accident. You were the passengers in the car that hit Tony. On the local radio this morning you have heard that Tony has come out of his coma.

The driver of the car is your older friend, Barry. He has a full driving licence, but when he caused the accident he had been drinking. In fact, he regularly takes his car out when he is drunk.

Are you going to do anything about this terrible accident?

Allow the groups time to organise themselves and improvise the scene once through. Share the improvisations to show the different attitudes to what happened.

What decisions does the group come to? Can they justify their course of action? Can they predict the consequences of their decision? Does the information that Tony is going to recover make any difference?

Activity A8: Recording the work

Using the improvisation as a basis, ask each group to script this short scene using the notation that they have learned in previous exercises. File the script as 'At the Bus Stop' in their group's file.

Activity A9

In the same groups, it is time to consider the consequences of your decision. First, discuss what might happen as a result of your actions. Then, devise a short scene that shows what happens.

- *If the friends decide to do nothing, what happens? Does Barry do something like this in the future? Does Barry end up killing someone, or himself?*
- *If you tell the police, what happens? Does it cause conflict because you have informed on a friend?*
- *If you confront Barry, what happens? Can you convince him to own up?*

Allow the groups time to prepare their scenes and then share them.

Activity A10: Recording the work

As this task is more composed, or 'polished', if possible arrange for each group to tape-record their dialogue. From this tape, ask them to transcribe a scene called 'Consequences'.

- *Are tape recording and transcription effective means of creating scripted drama?*
- *What are the possible problems associated with this method?*

Activity A11:   Reconciliation?

In their groups, ask students to consider what might happen if at some point in the future Barry met with Tony's parents. Would any kind of reconciliation be possible? Where might such an encounter take place? What other characters might be present?

Some suggestions:

- As part of a young offenders' programme aimed at getting offenders to face the consequences of their actions.
- As members of the public invited onto a TV 'chat show'.
- By accident – they happened to be on holiday in the same hotel.
- The encounter happens in the form of a dream or nightmare: Barry's? Or mum's/dad's?

Ask the groups to compose a short scene that demonstrates the difficulties faced by the characters in this encounter.

Activity A12:   Recording the work

Once more ask the group to record their scene.

By this stage in the unit all groups should now possess a file containing the following drafts of scenes:

- interesting or memorable phrases spoken by witnesses to the accident who were *hotseated* in activity A1;
- a draft of a short, naturalistic scene with stage directions titled 'The Hospital' from activity A2;
- versions of the scene arising from the forum theatre in activity A3;
- a draft of a short scene taking place 'at the bus stop' (activity A4);
- a draft script of a polished improvisation titled 'Consequences', based on what happened as a result of the previous decisions made by the characters (activity A5);
- a draft of a scene showing attempts at reconciliation between Barry and Tony's parents (activity A6).

Extension work

The students should now have drafted a series of scenes with dialogue, stage directions and a clear narrative. To verify this you may need to ask each group to read their script, scene by scene, in chronological order.

> *Playwrights often write scripts that are then received by actors and theatre companies who begin the process of staging the play. What are the difficulties faced by a writer who is composing a script to be performed by others? Alternatively, from the point of view of the actor, what are the difficulties in interpreting a script created by someone else?*

During the next phase of the work, the students will have the opportunity to re-draft their scripts using a range of workshop techniques, finally giving the opportunity for another group to act out their work.

At this stage encourage the groups to become active in planning a 'rehearsed reading' (ignore for a moment the material generated by activity A1).

Having 'walked through' the script, do the groups feel that their work communicates their intentions to an audience? What do they need to do in order to improve it?

Some questions:

- Is sufficient dramatic tension developed to keep the audience's interest? How might tension be focused in the scene(s)?

- Do we get to know enough about the key characters so as to care about what happens? What might need to be added in terms of action or dialogue in order to develop the characters?
- Does the structure of the embryonic play carry the narrative? How might altering the structure improve its clarity, or cause the action to unfold in a more interesting way?
- Are the students happy with their play as a vehicle to communicate their intentions? If not, how might its meaning be made clearer without becoming 'untheatrical' and obvious?

The task now is to help students begin the process of crafting the various draft elements of the 'work in progress' into a more coherent drama.

Suggested workshop activities:

- Redraft or add scenes. Students may work individually or in groups to change scenes or draft new ones. However, it should be emphasised that scenes should constantly be staged as part of an ongoing process so as to avoid the exercise becoming a creative writing task.
- Experiment with structure and chronology. By re-ordering the playing of scenes, a variety of interesting dramatic effects might be explored. The merits and demerits of each scene as a starting point for the play might be explored. Again, encourage the students to think in terms of the overall meaning of the piece for an audience. Other possibilities include the repeating of particular scenes or sequences, or the addition of narrative links or other forms of direct address.
- Adopt a framing device. By, for instance, beginning with the 'chat show' scene, and using the device of *flashback*, the subsequent action might become more significant by being so 'framed'. As a further example, utilising the fragments of dialogue recorded as 'the accounts of the eyewitness' in an early scene might have the effect of 'presenting' the whole play from the perspective of the eyewitness.
- Judge the effect of adding 'captions' or spoken titles to scenes, as in some forms of epic theatre. Alternatively, the newspaper report of the accident might itself be used in the drama in various ways. For example, what would be the contrasting effects of:

  (a) Using an OHP of the newspaper as a visual backdrop for the whole piece?
  (b) Presenting the newspaper story as a prologue to the drama?
  (c) Breaking the report into sections and using a section of it to introduce each scene?

Once groups are happy with their script, ask them to exchange it with another group. The script that they receive will now form the basis of their work towards performance. Asking groups to exchange these 'second draft' scripts before rehearsal should enable the students to take a more objective view of their work, and also allow them to 'test' the work that they have done – as a different group attempts to interpret it in performance.

SECTION B: *FINDERS KEEPERS* – SCRIPTING FOR TELEVISION AND FILM

In this second unit, students will use their improvised drama to create a simple screenplay for television or film. In television and film scripts writers have to provide information about the image that the camera will select for the viewer. 'Stage directions' are therefore often very detailed, and give a clear visual impression of the scene. The emphasis in this work is therefore to help students to understand how drama of this kind uses visual material in interesting ways to convey information about setting, narrative and character.

Activity B1

Have you ever found something that was valuable – perhaps money or jewellery? What should you do if you find something that does not belong to you? Sometimes there might be a temptation to keep whatever you have found, especially if there is no means of finding the rightful owner.

Form groups of three:

• Who are we?	Three teenage friends.
• Where are we?	On a bus.
• When are we?	Saturday morning, present day.

Ask the groups to label themselves A, B and C, and then brief the students separately:

- A: *You are a very honest person. You have always been taught that you should hand in anything that you find. For you, honesty is always the best policy.*
- B: *You feel that if you are given an opportunity, you should seize it. You believe, 'finders keepers, losers weepers'; their loss is your gain.*
- C: *You feel you should judge each situation upon its own merits. You are an honest person, but you will not pass up an opportunity if one presents itself.*

Once the students have been briefed, introduce the situation and ask them to change their working space so that it resembles the seats on a bus.

The three of you are travelling on the bus back from town where you have been shopping. It has been a good morning and you are discussing the things that you have bought.

Allow the students time to improvise the above for a few moments to establish their roles before stopping the whole group and giving the following information.

Suddenly, C notices a small packet lying on the floor of the bus, underneath one of the empty seats. It looks interesting and one of you picks it up. To your utter astonishment, it is a plastic envelope with ten tightly rolled twenty pound notes inside. There is also a slip of paper with an address written on it.

Allow the students time to run through the improvisation once. What do the friends decide to do? Share some of the improvisations and discuss the different responses.

Activity B2:   Recording the work

Before scripting the scene ask the students to plan out their 'screenplay' using a sequence of storyboards, using a separate A4 sheet of paper for each image. They should first of all seek to establish the setting for the scene as economically as possible. Ask the groups to consider the various 'camera shots' necessary to present the scene in a TV format. This exercise will also encourage students to think visually about their work. Creating visual representations of the various elements of the scene will also offer opportunities to discuss how particular information can be 'signed' to an audience – for instance, how a camera shot of a passing bus may signify that the subsequent action takes place *on* the bus.

Once this work is completed, students can draft the dialogue created during the improvisation, adding storyboards showing the visual image presented during each short section of dialogue.

In order to create a 'screenplay' for the scene – where the script is notated in words rather than pictures – ask students to insert stage directions between the dialogue which convey in words the visual impact of the scene. For example:

Exterior. Daytime. Establishing shot of busy city street. We see a passing double-decker bus.

Change of perspective, point of view from across the road. Traffic runs in and out of shot. Cut to wide shot of people waiting in line at a bus stop. We see our three characters joining the line, laughing and joking. We can't hear what they are saying over the traffic, but they are animated and lively. A bus pulls into shot.

Cut to establishing shot of bus interior. We see our three characters spread out on the rear couple of rows, comparing what they have bought: CDs, clothes, etc.

ANDREW:	Three quid off . . .!
BRIAN:	Let's have a look?

Close-up on Andrew's reaction.

ANDREW:	They're not fake, if that's what you think.

Cut to close-up on Brian.

BRIAN:	No? Real 'uns are thirty-five quid.

Wide shot showing whole group.

CARLA:	Leave him alone. You're only jealous!
BRIAN:	Not me. So what we doing later?
ANDREW:	Spent up.
CARLA:	I thought we were going to the pics?
ANDREW:	If you're payin'.

We are aware that BRIAN has not been following the previous exchange. He is looking elsewhere, down behind his seat.

Insert shot of what Brian has found from his point of view.

Cut to close up of Brian's face – pull out to include whole group.

BRIAN:	What the . . .? S' a wallet!

We see BRIAN open the wallet. Inside is a large wad of £20 notes, and a piece of paper.

BRIAN:	Geraldine Richards, 14 Cambridge Terrace . . .

Cut to medium shot

ANDREW and CARLA:	We're rich!

Fade out.

Students may find it helpful to use the above example as a starting point, and to write the final section of the scene showing the friends' reactions to the finding of the £200.

Activity B3

Some of the responses from the previous work might well form the basis of further improvisations. The learning area for the students should be to explore the repercussions of the characters' actions, and the way in which particular decisions could fundamentally affect a number of other people's lives. Here are some suggestions for further work:

- We see the person who has lost the £200. What does this mean to them? Are they wealthy or poor? Was the money to pay for something special? Students share their versions.
- We see the friends spending the money. Do they go on a spending spree? Are their intentions purely selfish or do they put the money to some other use?
- What happens if they decide to hand in the money? Does the rightful owner claim it? Do the friends receive a reward? How do they feel about being honest and handing in the money?

Activity B4: Recording the work

Ask the class how the action of these scenes might be communicated to a TV audience using only minimal dialogue. Again, begin the process using storyboards to create a visual 'map' for one of the scenes. If appropriate, add dialogue, as in the previous example, but encourage the students to think visually and to keep the dialogue to a minimum.

Activity B5

Form groups of three:

- Who are we?   The same three teenage friends.
- Where are we?   Outside the address specified on the slip of
                                                       paper found with the money.
- When are we?   Later that Saturday afternoon.

> *As the address on the slip of paper is nearby, you decide to go and have a look at the house. When you get to the street, you realise that it is a very wealthy area. The houses are enormous, with garages and drives; many with security gates to stop unwelcome guests. You soon find the house you are looking for. It is a very large house, with its own private drive. Obviously, the people who live here are very wealthy. As you watch from the road, a woman with two children comes out of the front door. After waving to someone still inside the house, she ushers the children into a silver Mercedes Benz, starts the engine and drives off down the road.*
>
> *Now you have seen the house on the address, what are you going to do with the money? Does it make any difference to your decision – knowing that £200 to these people would be a very small amount of money indeed?*

Allow the students time to plan their responses to this situation. What do the friends do next?

Activity B6: Recording the work

Ask the students to suggest a suitable location for the above scene. In order to 'set the scene' of this location for the viewer, what 'establishing shots' might be necessary? Could the entire narrative of this scene be communicated in visual terms, without dialogue?

Instruct the students to plot the scene in storyboard form. What is the minimum number of shots necessary?

Activity B7

After sharing some of the previous work, explain that you will be taking on a role in order to focus on two different responses to the situation. In the previous task it is likely that one of the groups will have come to the decision that they should approach the house and hand in the money. If not, volunteers could be asked for, to interact with the teacher in role.

Arrange the students into a semi-circle and improvise the two following situations with two groups of students while the others observe:

(a)   The friends decide to approach the house and hand in the money

As a group, you walk through the gates and up the drive to the front door of the house. You ring the bell and wait for a reply.

Assume the role of the home-owner: the money was indeed lost, but not by anyone in the family. You employ a cleaner to do the housework for a few days each week. The money found was their monthly wage.

(b)   The friends decide to leave and not hand in the money

Having made your decision, you turn to leave. As you do, you see an elderly woman approaching. She is obviously upset and looks quite distressed. She seems to be looking for something on the pavement as she walks towards you.

Assume the role of the cleaner. You are returning to the house to see if you have left your wages there. You need the money, as your pension does not go far enough each month. You think you may have dropped the money on the bus, but no one has handed it in at the bus station.

Leave time for reflection on the drama. What issues have been raised by the work?

Activity B8:   Recording the work

Ask each group to create an alternative ending for their screenplay, based upon their improvisations.

- Which ending is dramatically most effective?
- Is there a 'moral' implicit in their selected ending?

Viewing the 'screenplays' as a whole, what editing or redrafting is necessary? Ask groups to consider how their screenplay might actually translate to film or video. For instance, have they considered the number, sequence and duration of camera shots needed?

If technology allows, use the scripts as a basis for a 'shooting script' and record the work onto videotape. What issues are raised in transferring the drama from one medium to another?

DILEMMAS

Resource sheet 1

The Local Messenger

Hit and Run Horror

Local boy Tony Wells is recovering in hospital today after his horrific ordeal over the weekend. Tony was walking home on Friday night after spending the evening at a friend's house. As he crossed Rosamond Street, a hatchback car came speeding out of Derby Lane and hit Tony.

The force of the crash threw Tony onto the pavement, where he lay unconscious until medical help arrived. A local resident, who was walking his dog, saw the accident, but did not manage to identify the car before it drove off at speed, heading towards the city centre.

'All I heard was a screech of tyres and a very loud thump,' the witness said. 'The car had come to a standstill as if the driver was wondering what to do, then it simply sped off into the night.'

A police spokesperson added, 'We are obviously very pleased that Tony looks set to make a full recovery. But that does not take away from the fact that there is a driver out there who has little or no regard for other people who use our roads, or their lives. This could have been a tragedy, and someone knows who is responsible. We need to make sure that this driver does not do this sort of thing again.'

Tony, who celebrated his fourteenth birthday last week, was in a coma for two days. Although he is off the critical list, doctors at the hospital say that it will be many weeks before he makes a full recovery.

Anyone who has any information regarding this incident can contact their local police. Any information given will be treated in the strictest confidence.

DILEMMAS

Resource sheet 2

Script notation

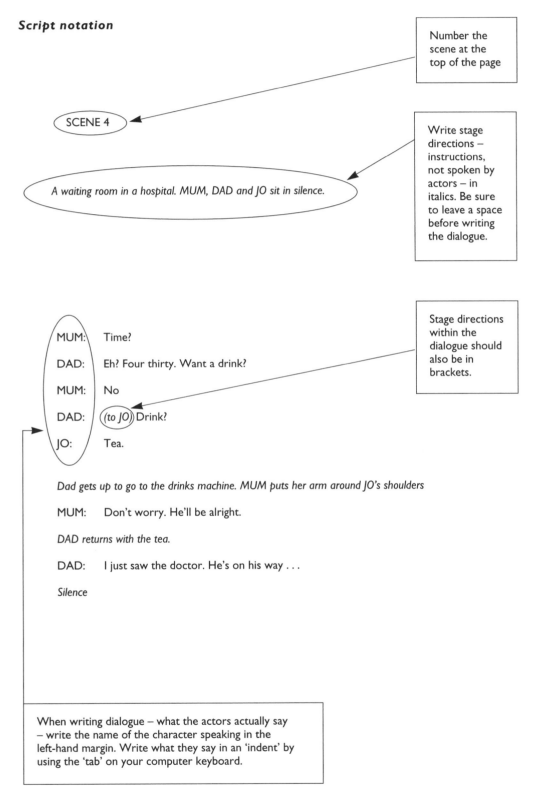

Number the scene at the top of the page

Write stage directions – instructions, not spoken by actors – in italics. Be sure to leave a space before writing the dialogue.

Stage directions within the dialogue should also be in brackets.

SCENE 4

A waiting room in a hospital. MUM, DAD and JO sit in silence.

MUM: Time?

DAD: Eh? Four thirty. Want a drink?

MUM: No

DAD: *(to JO)* Drink?

JO: Tea.

Dad gets up to go to the drinks machine. MUM puts her arm around JO's shoulders

MUM: Don't worry. He'll be alright.

DAD returns with the tea.

DAD: I just saw the doctor. He's on his way . . .

Silence

When writing dialogue – what the actors actually say – write the name of the character speaking in the left-hand margin. Write what they say in an 'indent' by using the 'tab' on your computer keyboard.

Unit 3

Displaced people

Introduction and context

As a signatory of the 1951 United Nations Convention on Refugees and the 1967 Protocol, the United Kingdom, along with all UN member states, has an international obligation to provide a safe haven for those fleeing torture, persecution or death, regardless of their nationality.

The issue of 'displaced people' is a major global concern. According to Amnesty International, a new refugee is made every 21 seconds and it is estimated that one in every 115 people on earth has been forced into flight at some time. The United Nations High Commission for Refugees (UNHCR) estimates that there are 27 million people in the world who are 'of concern' to them. Although worldwide most refugees are women and children, the majority of asylum seekers to Europe and North America are men. Their image is often shaped by a combination of ignorance, prejudice and misinformation.

In February 2002, a study by the European Monitoring Centre on Racism and Xenophobia set out to assess how negative and positive portrayals of refugees in the media influenced public opinion. The results highlighted that the British media's representation of asylum seekers is particularly negative and placed Britain as one of Europe's most hostile nations towards asylum issues. Within the study, there are warnings for all European countries that might have cultivated a sense of complacency derived from the fact that 80 per cent of the world's refugee population live outside Europe and North America (Amnesty International, 2003).

The term 'asylum seeker' is used to describe someone who has to flee his or her country because of violence or persecution. In this project, we use accounts from real asylum seekers that illustrate the often-shocking circumstances of their flight. Acknowledging the fact that students might initially have negative attitudes towards such people, we have chosen to address the topic directly as opposed to a more metaphorical or analogous treatment. We hope that by allowing the students to experiment with the real words of refugees, the humanity behind the familiar – and often negative – media headlines is made a little clearer.

For many asylum seekers already within the processing system of a host country, telling their story becomes a principal element of coming to terms with their situation. To reflect this, the work explores narrative and storytelling, encouraging the students to experiment with different forms and styles that create a specific experience for both the performer and the audience. The work also poses questions as to the responsibilities dramatists and theatre practitioners have in interpreting real events that have happened to real people.

We anticipate that a group exploring all the activities in this unit would take about seven one-hour lessons to complete the tasks.

Displaced People **unit map**

Activity	Description	Resources	Teacher notes
Activity 1	'Home' and 'country' brainstorms.		
Activity 2	Soundscapes of home.		
Activity 3	Newspaper article; welfare team in Seaville: meeting – action plan.	Resource sheet 1	
Activity 4	Teacher in role as Nico.		
Activity 5	Interviews 'to camera' with residents.		
Activity 6	Reconvened welfare team meeting: teacher in role as residents 'invited in'. Team reconsider.	Resource sheet 2	
Activity 7	'Carrier bag' exercise.	Plastic carrier bags; slips of paper	
Activity 8	Border crossing: teacher in role as guard.		
Activity 9	Dramatising refugees' testimony: narration conventions.	Resource sheet 3	
Activity 10	Add fictional scenes to sequence.		
Activity 11	Arrival at immigration control: interviews.		
Activity 12	*The Bogus Woman* extract: annotated script; stage the scene.	Resource sheet 4	
Activity 13	Reflection: the final destination.		

Activity 1

Explain to the students that the drama will explore a number of different drama techniques and both you and the students will be taking on roles. You may wish to introduce the idea that the work will also focus upon narrative and how we re-tell stories and interpret real events that are happening now or have happened in the past.

Write the word 'home' on the board.

- *What does the word 'home' mean to you?*
- *What feeling or emotions do you associate with the word 'home'?*
- *How would you feel if you were forced to leave your home forever?*

Now write the words 'your country' on the board.

- *What do the words 'your country' mean to you?*
- *How important is your country in shaping who you are?*
- *How would you feel if you were made to leave your country forever?*
- *What do we call someone who has been forced to leave his or her country because of war or conflict, political belief or religion?*

Explain that the drama work is going to examine some of the ideas around the themes of home and country. You might wish to raise the theme of refugees now, or allow the students to make their own links as the work progresses.

Activity 2

This exercise explores different concepts of 'home'. Explain that, in small groups, they are going to create a soundscape. Ask the students to list the types of noises and sounds they might hear in an ordinary house or home. Allocating five minutes for the task, tell them to recreate these different sounds and pieces of dialogue and build them up as a collage. Remind them that their soundscape does not have to tell a story or have a plot, it should simply be layers of sounds or words that convey a sense of 'home'.

Share each group's work.

- *Did they manage to capture the essence of home life?*
- *What sounds, noises or words were the most effective?*
- *When using this technique, what role does the audience have in making the images 'come to life'?*

Explain that they will be returning to this exercise later in the project.

Activity 3

Read out the newspaper article *End of the Line for Refugees* (Resource sheet 1, page 78) and introduce the next phase of the work by explaining that everyone is going to take on a role. Set the context of the work by telling the students the following:

• Who are we?	Council workers in Seaville, responsible for the welfare of the refugees due to arrive in the town.
• Where are we?	In the local civic hall.
• When are we?	Present day, in the evening.
• What are we doing?	Being briefed by the council leader (teacher in role).

Ask the group to arrange their chairs in a suitable layout for a formal group meeting. Once the students have defined the space, tell them the work will begin when you start the meeting in role. Tack the newspaper article to the board.

> *As council leader for Seaville, I would like to welcome you – the newly appointed welfare team – whose job it is to ensure that these refugees settle in Seaville as quickly as possible.*
>
> *As you know, the town is to play host to around 400 refugees who are fleeing persecution, torture or war in their own countries. As yet, it is unclear whether their requests for political asylum will be granted; some of them may well be going back to where they came from. Needless to say, these people have been through a great deal and, although this situation may put a strain upon our already stretched social and public services, it is our job to resolve any problems or conflicts which may arise in the next few months.*
>
> *As you may be aware, there have been some reports in the local press, and there may be opposition from the local community.*
>
> *What we have to do now is compose an action plan. Perhaps a good place to start would be to consider any potential problems that might be faced by our visitors, and then propose solutions to those problems. Any thoughts?*

Allow the discussion to unfold. Care may be needed at this point to ensure that the discussion stays focused and does not become a general debate on the rights and wrongs of immigration in general. Through the convention of *mantle of the expert* the students need to consider the community's possible negative reactions to playing host to a group of people who are in the process of making a claim for political asylum, and devise solutions for addressing those concerns. The following information from you will add more context to the work:

- A disused hospital will be refurbished and made suitable to use as a centre to house most of the asylum seekers; others will be staying in bed and breakfast accommodation.
- Asylum seekers might be able to claim some benefits while they await decisions on their appeal for asylum.
- The children will be integrated into local schools.
- It is uncertain how long these people will be here.
- Interpreters will be on hand to help with any language problems.

Activity 4

> *So as to assist you in your work, I'd like to introduce you to Nico. Nico is a refugee who has been in the country for a year now, and speaks good English. In his home country he was persecuted and was in grave danger. He's been through a lot, and he's come along to help us understand something of the type of people we'll be helping. Before we bring Nico in, what kinds of questions might we want to ask him?*

Compile a list of questions that the group wants to put to Nico, before explaining that you will now switch roles. It may be helpful here to use one or more *role signifiers* – a scarf or jacket, perhaps – to clarify the transition between teacher/council leader/Nico.

Assume the role of Nico, and allow the students – still in role as council workers – to question you. As you already know the questions they are going to ask you should be able to 'prepare' your responses.

Giving the students an opportunity to question Nico should:

- allow them to 'rehearse' their roles as council welfare workers;
- reinforce the urgency of the situation and the size of the problem that faces them;
- clarify the important point that the people they are to assist are fleeing from serious situations and are in danger.

At the end of the episode, come out of role as Nico.

As council leader once more, reconvene the welfare team meeting. Ask the students to reflect on their encounter with Nico: what has the team learned that might assist them in their task?

In your role as facilitator, suggest that it will be important for the team to undertake some research amongst the people of Seaville. Conclude the discussion by suggesting that one way of gauging public opinion would be to conduct a survey of the views of the local residents. Allow the welfare team to compose four or five questions that might form the core of an interview with a sample of local people.

Activity 5

Ask the students to form groups of four. Using the questionnaire as a starting point, each group has to dramatise the responses of four different residents. Encourage the students to explore a wide range of people, who might offer very different responses. Before they start work, tell the groups that there is no need to portray the interviewer, as this work will be presented as a series of short responses as if 'to camera'. Placing a single stool or chair for the students to sit on centrally – as if in a video booth – might frame their monologues. After allowing a few minutes for the groups to prepare their improvisations, share some or all of the work.

Activity 6

Evaluate the responses by re-convening the meeting and, in role as the welfare team, reflect upon the points made by the residents. Do the responses largely reflect the earlier discussion by the welfare team? Does the team now have to re-assess its planning in the light of the strength of negative or positive feelings voiced by the residents?

In role as the council leader, address the group:

> Perhaps the next step is to invite some of these local people in to speak to us directly. We might be able to answer their questions or reassure them if necessary. Who should we choose?

From the suggestions made by the group, the teacher now selects one or more roles to adopt in front of the welfare team. In this way the teacher in role, rather than a student, is able to voice the concerns of the local residents and encourage the students to consider ways of responding to those concerns in a positive light. This is a challenging task and your students may need some help as they come to recognise that the task of reassuring a community might be a difficult one. Recognising the difficulty of finding 'solutions' to such a complex issue, it would certainly be appropriate to stop the role work and, using Resource sheet 2 (page 79), discuss the reasons why such a community might be defensive.

Activity 7

Explain that the next exercise will take place within a strict time limit and that the context of the work has now changed and is no longer set in Seaville. Place the students into groups of five. On the floor in front of each group place a marker, ten slips of paper and a plastic carrier bag. Now introduce the task by reading out or adapting the opening teacher statement.

> The groups that you are in represent a family. You must remember that you must cater for the needs of each family member as you attempt this task. Although you can take on the roles of children, any role you choose should be old enough to participate fully in the drama work.
>
> Listen very carefully to what I am going to say, you will hear these instructions only once.
>
> You must leave your homes. Your family is in great danger. Your country has been invaded and the advancing army is reputed to be killing everyone in its path. There are no communication links to the outside world, your telephones and mobiles do not work. There is no television or radio, no

Internet or e-mail. Petrol and fuel stations have been seized. Banks have closed and all trading has been frozen. The police and emergency services have ceased to operate.

You have ten minutes to leave your homes. You can take only what you can carry in your carrier bags. You are encouraged to head for open ground where there is less chance of being caught by hostile soldiers. You goal is to reach the border checkpoint and pass through to the safety of a neighbouring country that has promised to let in a small number of refugees. It might be some time before aid agencies will reach you, so you are advised to take items that might help you survive in the open.

To represent what you are taking, write each article down on the slip of paper provided and place it in your bag. You have ten minutes to complete this task. Your time starts now.

As the groups negotiate what they are going to put in their carrier bags you will need to build a sense of tension and urgency to complete the task. By circulating around the groups and employing careful questioning you will be able to encourage your students to consider their choices: how useful or practical are the items they have included?

The students need to consider the following:

- *What time of year is it?*
- *What about papers and official documents such as birth certificates and passports?*
- *What use are chequebooks or credit cards if the banks are closed?*
- *Is there any cash in the house?*
- *What about food or fresh water?*
- *What about toiletries?*
- *What if they need to make a fire or build a shelter in the open?*

Once the time is up, ask each group to put their bags on the floor in front of them and listen to the following context.

Your family decides to follow the advice you have been given and you leave your homes, heading for open countryside and the nearby border crossing point. As you walk, you join hundreds of other families who are all doing exactly the same thing as you. As the crowds swell, rumours of shooting and violence circulate and you imagine you hear the roar of helicopters overhead and the sporadic chatter of rifle fire in the distance.

By the time you approach the border crossing, the crowd you are in numbers tens of thousands. Another rumour reaches you through the crowd. It is the hostile army that has control of the border. The border is heavily fortified and armed guards are evident. You will have to pass through them to reach the safety of the other side. You join the growing queue of refugees and wait.

Activity 8

Using two chairs or stage blocks, create an opening that represents the border checkpoint. Tell the groups that you are going to take on the role of the border guard. Choose a group to be the first family attempting to pass through the barrier. The role the teacher plays is a high status, controlling role and you should emphasise to the students that, within the context of the drama, there is no room for challenging or inappropriate behaviour.

Ask the first group to approach the control point, then immediately challenge them to halt and present their belongings. It is up to the teacher in role as to how the border guard interacts with each family, but the following suggestions might be useful:

- Find the piece of paper that says 'passports' and confiscate it.
- Find any cash or money that might be in the bag and confiscate it.
- Ask individuals to remove their jewellery or watches and confiscate them.
- Remove one member of the group and send them to wait in another line.
- Confiscate any weapons or items that might be used as weapons.

- Present the opportunity for the family to offer bribes.
- Allow a family to pass unimpeded.

As each family watches the previous family go through the border, they will anticipate the requests of the guard and may attempt different ploys to get past with as many of their belongings intact as possible. If you find students challenging your actions or status, stop the drama and come out of role. Remind the students of the refugees' vulnerability and the danger of their situation. Another effective strategy is to freeze the group into a still image and use narration as a control device:

> *Under the watchful eyes of the armed soldiers in the watchtower, the guard then searches every member of the group and confiscates your passports. The family is then allowed to cross the border.*

Once all the groups have experienced attempting to cross the checkpoint, it is important to allow time to evaluate and discuss the work:

- *What did it feel like to be so powerless?*
- *How did the families feel about losing their important documents or passports? Why were these taken?*
- *Do they think they will ever see their valuables or belongings again?*
- *Is it a relief to be out of danger? Are they out of danger?*
- *What do the families feel about the immediate future?*
- *How do they feel about being forced out of their own country?*
- *Do they think they will ever be able to return to their country?*

Activity 9

In the following section, the students will work to dramatise extracts from the testimony of real displaced people. This dramatisation will represent the exile, journey and arrival of a group of refugees. As you prepare to share the extracts with the students, you should stress that the stimulus for the drama work is now shifting focus. Whereas the previous work was based on imaginary situations, the following drama tasks are based on real words recorded from real refugees. The work will also allow the students to investigate the use of the narrator in drama.

Write the words 'narration' and 'narrator' on the board:

- *If someone is a narrator in a play, what do they do?*
- *Narration can be used in a simple or complicated way. A simple use of a narrator would be to help tell a story to an audience. A more sophisticated use of narration might involve indicating a character's state of mind or emotions, presenting a scene or setting, a theme or topic or an abstract element that is not immediately apparent or clear to the audience.*
- *Narration creates a specific relationship with the performers and the action, and the performers and the audience.*
- *Narration is a common technique in the arts – can anyone describe an example from theatre, film, radio, literature or television that uses narration?*

The *narrative conventions* table is provided as a comprehensive guide to the different ways that this technique might be employed, and to the different dramatic effects that can be produced.

Divide the class into groups of four or five. Distribute copies of Resource sheet 3 (page 80) and, as a whole group, read through the extracts. The group will need time to discuss and reflect upon the implications of the experiences recounted, and encouraging the students to empathise with the plight of the young people who have written the accounts will add depth and meaning to their drama work. Explain that the drama work will offer opportunities to experiment with simple narration techniques, and by exploring the use of various forms of narration they will recognise that subtly different dramatic effects are possible through fairly simple means.

Some narrative conventions

Narrative form	Past or present tense?	First, second or third person	Relationships: audience/other performers	Perspective	Dramatic effect
Voiceover	Past	Third	No physical presence on stage. Audience hear narrative as disembodied voice: presence of narrator not acknowledged by performers.	One who knows what happened or has insight into the characters' thoughts or feelings. *Julia walked the streets of the city ...she didn't know who to turn to ... until there, in a café, was Mike....*	Narrator – a disembodied voice – appears to have a controlling function – from outside the action. Can move narrative forward or elucidate subtext. A cinematic convention rarely used in live theatre.
Voiceover – commentator	Present	Third	No physical presence on stage. Audience hear narrative as disembodied voice: narration not acknowledged by performers.	One who has insight into the characters' thoughts or feelings as events are unfolding. *Julia walks on, trying to make sense of what she sees about her.*	Narrative is again outside the action, but the effect is more immediate. A cinematic convention rarely used in live theatre.
Voiceover – conscience	Past	First or second	No physical presence on stage. Audience hear narrative as disembodied voice: narration not acknowledged by performers.	The voice of one of the characters able to give their own perspective, insight or thoughts on the action with the benefit of hindsight. *I walked into the café – and there was Mike. He looked glad to see me.*	We are being given information unknown to the other characters. A cinematic convention rarely used in live theatre.
Voiceover – here and now	Present	First or second	Audience hear narrative as disembodied voice: presence of narrator not acknowledged by performers.	The voice of one of the characters, able to give their own perspective, insight or thoughts on the action as it unfolds. *As I walk into the café, the place falls silent. My companion and I begin to feel uneasy.*	We are being given a commentary on the action from the perspective of those involved. A cinematic convention rarely used in live theatre.

continued

Some narrative conventions (continued)

Narrative form	Past or present tense?	First, second or third person	Relationships: audience/ other performers	Perspective	Dramatic effect
Storyteller	Past	Third	Narrator present on stage, literally recounting or retelling a story to an audience: direct address. Does not normally acknowledge the presence of other performers. Many possible proxemic relationships with other performers on stage, and these can provide subtle nuances. The relationship with the audience is important. The storyteller can be neutral, conspirator, confident or controller of the audience/action.	Let me tell you . . . A 'conventional' narrator, outside the story, relating it to an audience. Once upon a time A time of bloodshed When this city was called the city of the damned It had a Governor . . .' (Brecht: The Caucasian Chalk Circle.)	We are being told a story from the past. Open, flexible convention, which allows the narrator to 'know what is about to happen' or provide insight into characters' motivation or thoughts. Experimenting with spatial arrangements can determine meaning: a book can 'come to life' or the narrator can 'make the story happen'.
Commentator	Present	Third	Narrator present on stage, literally relating events to an audience as they happen: direct address. Does not normally acknowledge the presence of performers.	Commentator, outside the action. As she walks through the streets, she hears her name being called . . .	We are being told about – or shown – something as it happens. The narrator can provide immediate insight into characters' motivation or thoughts.
Anecdotal/ autobiographical	Past	First or second	Narrator tells of events that happened to him or her. Direct address to audience. May acknowledge performers – sometimes one of the performers will portray the narrator in the drama.	Raconteur, remembering the past. Let me tell you what happened when my friends and I left the café . . .	Personal perspective provided on past events – from the inside. Can be very involving for an audience.

Technique	Tense	Person	Description	Example	Effect
Here and now	Present	First or second	Narrator relates events to the audience as they happen. Narrator is the voice of the performer.	It is happening to me now. *We go into the room. It is dark; I hear a voice. . . .*	Immediate, urgent, direct communication; we hear and see things as they are happening.
Controller	Present tense intervention in a past tense narrative	Third	Narrator interacts with performers – often by 'freezing' the action to allow analysis or reflection.	I am the author of this story and I have power over the characters. *(Freeze) At this point let us pause to consider what other options were available to Oliver.*	Provides a reflexive perspective on the drama. The narrator appears to be responsible for the drama.
Self-narration ('shared experience')	Either past or present: can switch from one to other	Switches from third to first or second person	Performer is both outside narrator and character in the drama and changes from one to the other often and rapidly.	I am an actor and this is a story. I can present action (in role) and provide narration (out of role) simply by switching rapidly from one to the other. *James put down his bags with a flourish and said: (as James:) 'How do you do, Aunt?' He waited for the inevitable reply.*	Explicit, self-reflexive storytelling device: enables small casts to enact large-scale dramas by switching characters rapidly.
Stepping out of the action	Can switch from present (action) to past (narration)	Switches from first person (character) to third (narrator)	Performer can stop being the character to narrate.	Sometimes I will step out of my role to narrate. *James: 'How do you do Aunt?' (Actor steps forward). Narrator: James put down his bags and awaited the inevitable reply. Meanwhile in the next room something sinister was happening . . .*	Explicitly theatrical reflexive device: 'distanced' or objective means of dealing with emotive material. Performer has joint role.
Aside	Either: usually present	Third	Changes from audience 'eavesdropping' on action to direct address, and back again. Actor steps out of the action to narrate or comment. Other performers are not aware of his/her commentary.	I am allowed to say things to you that they can't hear. *'Hello, George old friend!' (to audience:) 'What on earth is he wearing?'*	Explicitly theatrical device. Can provide insight and awareness of 'subtext': often highly comic.

Make clear to the groups that they must use the language of the extracts as narration, and must select appropriate dramatic action to 'illustrate' the text. The pieces of text can be broken down in various ways, and a pathway through the work might look like this:

- Each group reads their section of text. As they read, they should note the following: Who is speaking? What other characters are presented or implied in the text? Are there any clues as to setting? What is the mood or atmosphere of the passage? What feelings are described?
- Groups break down the text into sentences, or short sections. Are there any striking images in the section? What action is described? What are the key moments in the text that could be presented? How best might the group present these moments?
- The teacher presents each group with a particular narrative convention to employ in their dramatisation. Using the conventions table, the key elements of how the narrative is presented are clearly explained to the students.
- Groups then apply these conventions and highlight the sections of text spoken by each narrator or character, and include significant stage directions.
- As the groups complete their work, fit the scenes together, paying attention to the moments of transition from one section to the next. When performing a sequential drama of this sort each group takes its cue to begin from the group before it, and it is therefore important that groups clearly mark the end of their sequence – possibly with a still image or by consciously stepping 'in' and 'out' of the action.

Once the whole sequence has been prepared, the dramas are performed as a sequence in a negotiated order as 'work in progress'. The work can be enhanced – even at this relatively early stage – by carefully chosen sound, music or lighting. Evaluate the drama by considering:

- How far is the group satisfied that they have captured the feeling and meaning of their individual text?
- Have they created enough dramatic tension to make the work interesting for an audience? If not, how might the work be enhanced by the use of pauses or silence; contrasts or surprises; enhanced atmosphere or mood?
- In what way did the different narration conventions enhance or impede the drama? Was there a particularly successful example? What made it effective?
- How far have groups been able to stick to the 'real' action as described? What problems were encountered in doing this?

Activity 10

Once the overall drama sequence has been established and performed, the groups now have the opportunity to enhance their drama through the imaginative recreation of other, fictional, events, which may have occurred during the refugees' journeys. Each group now prepares a second scene that is devised using one of these titles:

- A moment of danger
- A moment of kindness
- A moment of hope
- A moment of despair
- A moment of longing
- A moment of celebration

The class may again wish to use narration, perhaps focusing on a convention they saw being employed by a different group. Of course, this time they will need to script the narrative themselves.

Explain that each group will eventually be responsible for two scenes – one dramatised extract and one fictional episode. Allow the students time to shape their dramas. Once rehearsed, an order of performance can be negotiated. This will involve cross-cutting from one scene to the next – not necessarily in any chronological order – until the most dramatically effective sequence is found. Again, groups may wish to select appropriate music, lighting or sound effects to enhance their work.

This section of work can lead to a substantial performance that bears scrutiny in its own right. Inviting in an audience to see this work – perhaps a younger Citizenship or PSHE class – would be appropriate. Capturing the work on video also allows detailed reflection on the work for those taking part:

- Was the work effective? Why?
- What did the group feel about using the real testimony of refugees in their dramatisation?
- What was the difference between the 'real' and 'fictional' sequences?
  What was the effect of juxtaposing the two?
- What effect did the various kinds of narration employed have? How did they:

  o   change the relationship with the audience;
  o   make the text more dramatic or give it more impact;
  o   make the drama seem more objective or 'factual'?

Activity 11

Ask the group what might happen once the refugees arrive in their country of destination – in this case the students' own country:

- *Would the refugees be simply 'allowed in' to the country?*
- *What might be the refugees' state of mind after their journey?*

Ask the class to re-form the groups they worked in during the border control drama (Activity 6). Explain that after a long and often dangerous journey, their group has arrived at their final host nation. This is where they will make their request for political asylum.

Ask each family group to form a still image of the moment of their arrival at immigration control. They are queuing to be interviewed by officials. As the students hold their tableaux, ask the students to speak their character's thoughts at this moment. It will be helpful for the concluding activities if these responses are recorded either by you or the students.

Out of role, give the group the following information:

> *You only have your carrier bags of belongings from the first exercise, but you are lucky – your group has managed to stay together. Each family must now select one person who is prepared to answer some routine questions . . .*

Ask the volunteers from each family to come forward. Explain that each person is taken to a separate room and interviewed at length by an official. Highlight the importance of this initial interview as the means by which the claims of the family are judged. Explain also that the interview might be conducted through an interpreter, be held at the end of a long journey, and that the claimant would be expected to detail exactly what had happened to them and why they in particular were in danger and could not return to their own country. Make clear that this is just the start of the immigration process, but a crucial one, and details missed here could well result in a valid application being turned down.

Activity 12

The group will now have the opportunity to examine how a playwright has chosen to deal with similar themes.

Kay Adshead, in her play *The Bogus Woman*, tells the story of a young woman's exile from her home in Africa, where she has worked as a journalist covering human rights issues. She receives threats from the military, and narrowly escapes a horrific attack in which her family and her young child, Anele, are brutally murdered in front of her. In the sequence reproduced in Resource sheet 4 (page 82), taken from the beginning of the play, the woman first arrives in England.

Distribute copies of the extract to the group and, having read through the text, ask the group to identify:

- *What is interesting about the way this scene is written?*
- *Why might the playwright have chosen to write in this way?* (The play is written for a solo performer, and in later scenes the young woman tells her story by enacting the roles of all other characters.)
- *Consider the opening words of the young woman: is she referring to the plane she is on as it lands, or is there a more symbolic meaning behind the words?*
- *How does the playwright convey a sense of the isolation and vulnerability of the woman through the language and staging?*

Ask the students to work in pairs. In order to clarify the scene, ask each pair to make up the questions to which the young woman is responding. They should consider who might be asking these questions, and the tone of the interview. This should also have the effect of encouraging the students to consider carefully how the woman responds to her interrogator.

After they have annotated their script, each pair should experiment with acting out this version of the scene. Share some of the work and discuss whether this has helped to clarify the scene.

Working in the same pairs, ask the students to return to the original text and rehearse a presentation of Kay Adshead's original sequence. The non-acting student should direct their partner. Remind them to consider how the playwright conveys the isolation and vulnerability of the young woman through the language and the staging. What clues are there to her feelings during different sections of the scene? Ask each pair to consider the staging of the scene and the audience configuration that might best suit such an intimate play. Encourage the students to consider design elements such as lighting or sound that might enhance the action. How would the following lighting effects work in performance?

- top lighting – a single, hard spotlight forming a circle around the actor;
- front lighting – a single, hard spotlight focused upon the top half or face of the actor;
- colour – different colours to signify the ambiguous opening and the reality of landing and subsequent interview.

Activity 13

The following reflective exercises should encourage the students to consider the themes of the drama, their personal viewpoint and the manner in which their viewpoint may have changed during the course of the work.

Divide the class into two groups. Ask each group to form a line or 'corridor', facing each other. Explain that you will be taking on the role of an asylum seeker symbolically making the last few steps of their journey – a journey that ends in a coastal town called Seaville. Once you have chosen a focus from the following suggestions, the students can address their words or phrases to this character as they walk along the 'corridor':

- *Knowing what you now know about refugees and asylum seekers, imagine that you have only a few minutes to leave your home. What would you take? Say these words as I pass along the corridor.*
- *Knowing what you now know about refugees and asylum seekers, what advice would you give someone in this position as they arrive in a new country? Say these words as I pass along the corridor.*

- *Remind yourself of the questions you composed during the previous script exercise exploring the play* The Bogus Woman. *Choose one of these lines, phrases or words to say as I pass along the corridor.*
- *As the asylum seekers arrive in Seaville, the local newspaper covers the story. Compose the headline from that edition and say it aloud as I pass along the corridor.*

DISPLACED PEOPLE

Resource sheet 1

Seaville Messenger

End of the line for Refugees

Beauty spot holiday town set for long-term guests

Government plans announced yesterday shockingly put the holiday town of Seaville on the map – as a holding centre for hundreds of refugees. The initiative will take place almost immediately in an attempt to hit challenging government targets by fast-tracking hundreds of asylum seekers through the processing system.

Inevitably the move has been criticised by some in the town for the potential strain it could inflict on local public services such as health care, housing and schools. A Government spokesperson commented, 'Although we appreciate the concerns of the local community, we all have to do our bit. This is a national issue and it is not something that is simply going to go away by ignoring it or pretending that it is not happening. Many of these people are desperate and need our help.'

The spokesperson went on to add that the move should not be seen as a permanent solution, and that many of the families were awaiting final decisions about their right to political asylum. In some cases this can take up to three years, although a recent review of the procedures was trying to have the process shortened to six months.

DISPLACED PEOPLE

Resource sheet 2

Myth

Asylum seekers see Britain as the land of milk and honey.

The facts

Asylum seekers are not allowed to claim mainstream welfare benefits. If they are destitute, the only option for some is to apply for support with the National Asylum Support Service (NASS), the Government department responsible for supporting destitute asylum applicants. NASS support is very basic indeed. A single adult has to survive on £37.77 a week – 30 per cent below the poverty line.

Myth

Asylum seekers are conmen.

The facts

Statistics published by the Home Office (2nd quarter, 2002) show that well over 50 per cent of asylum seekers are given permission to stay in this country.

Myth

Asylum seekers are illegal.

The facts

By definition, there is no such thing as an 'illegal asylum seeker'. The UK has signed the 1951 Convention on Refugees, which means that anyone has the right by law to apply for asylum in the UK and remain until a final decision on their asylum application has been made.

Myth

Asylum seekers are criminals.

The facts

According to the Association of Chief Police Officers (ACPO), asylum seekers are more likely to become victims of crime in the UK than UK citizens. There have been numerous attacks on asylum seekers around Britain, including the murder of asylum seekers in Glasgow and in Sunderland.

Myth

Asylum seekers are swamping Britain.

The facts

Even within the EU, the UK ranked 10th in terms of asylum applications in relation to the overall population in 2001. A MORI poll showed that people vastly overestimate the numbers of asylum seekers and refugees in the UK. On average people think that 23 per cent of the world's refugees and asylum seekers are in the UK, more than 10 times greater than the reality, which is actually less than 2 per cent.

DISPLACED PEOPLE

Resource sheet 3

(All extracts used by permission of The Refugee Council.)

Extract 1: Shpend (17 years old)

> The Serbs came to our house and threatened to kill us all. They beat us up – me not so much, but my father was badly injured. They told us we shouldn't be there, that we should get out. We left our house and went to live in the woods. We were there for two months. We lived in tents – we were only able to eat when our cousins brought food from the villages. While we were there, the police and army came and burnt our houses.

Extract 2: Renovat (age unknown)

> In 1993 some of our neighbours started stealing our families' goats, cows and crops. One night people came with axes and knives, so we ran away with some other neighbours. My grandparents were so old they could not run and escape. They were killed and houses were burned by people who were once my friends.

Extract 3: Sado (8 years old)

> I came back from Sunday school and I remember seeing that our living room as well as our kitchen had collapsed. Then I saw tanks in front of our house and they began firing. It was terrible. We ran as fast as we could, my mother holding my hand. There was also Feriyo, my friend, as well as her granny who was running behind us because she could not catch up with us. She was old . . . Feriyo fell down while we were still running and there was this deafening noise. I let go of my mother's hand and ran back to help Feriyo but she wouldn't stand up. I shook her, saying, 'Feriyo, stand up'. I begged her to stand but she wouldn't.

Extract 4: Wali (10 years old)

> One night some men came to our house and took my father away and he was shot. After that our life became very hard. I was woken up by a noise one morning at about four or five. My mother and my family went in to the corridors . . . and watched the rockets. They came four at a time . . . After this there were lots of soldiers walking about. Sometimes there were bad soldiers who went into houses and took things. All the schools were shut. I couldn't go to see my friends because it wasn't safe to go outside. The only time my mother went outside was to get food. After living like this for a week, my family decided we had to leave.

Extract 5: Choman (18 years old)

I was so enthusiastic about starting school and learning English . . . It was very hard. Some people treated me like a fool because I couldn't speak English well; some just ignored me as if I didn't exist. I was shocked to find out that in the lunch queue they used to laugh at me and say that I never had decent food in my country. They said I had always been hungry and that's why I ran away from my home. Nobody wanted to sit next to me in lessons and nobody wanted to have me as their partner in PE. I was all alone in the corner and did not understand the jokes during the lessons. I was too scared to talk in lessons because I knew that if I made a mistake some of them would laugh at me. Once I even got beaten up by a group of students who used to bully everyone. They said they couldn't stand me because I was a refugee who lived on the Government's money . . .

Extract 6: David (15 years old)

We were kept naked in cells. There were many other men in the same cell as me. It was very dirty and I developed a skin rash from all the mosquito bites. We had to sleep on the floor in rows and if you complained the guards would beat you . . . I just wanted to be safe.

DISPLACED PEOPLE

Resource sheet 4

Extract from *The Bogus Woman* by Kate Adshead

A large aircraft landing.

Airport ambience.

Lights snap up.

YOUNG BLACK WOMAN, *made up and in a*
pretty cotton frock with a hold-all, stands.

YOUNG WOMAN:
No, no,
up, up,
not down,
not here,
she's not here,
no-one's here.
Go up
Back to the clouds,
Up to Anele!
But it's cold,
Colder than here,
She'll need the shawl.

Frantically she empties the bag looking for the
shawl.

My mother made it
from white spit
and silver hair,
and ivory years.

I must go back up to the clouds
back up to my people.

(Sharply) Don't tell me what to do!
Take your hand off my arm!
Yes I have a passport.
I don't know,
in my bag.

I . . ., I . . .
I don't know my name.

(Quickly) You heard me.

I don't know which flight
I can't remember.
I don't know
where from,
you tell me.

No, I have no family in England.

(Quicker still, the words spilling out.) I told you
in my bag! I told you in my bag!

No I'm not on holiday!

No I've no-one meeting me!

No I'm not staying with friends!

I don't know yet!

Does it matter?

Does it matter?

Lights change.

Next stop . . . high school

A group-devised performance project

Introduction and context

This project provides a highly structured approach to devising and creating performance through improvisation. It allows a group of GCSE students the chance to produce a performance for a defined group of younger students. In particular, the question of finding an appropriate theatre style for this kind of 'didactic' drama is introduced, and opportunities to explore the relationship between performer and audience are provided. Students will also be presented with different approaches to characterisation including the deliberate use of stereotypes and 'stock characters'.

By capitalising upon the previous experience of the drama students, the play focuses upon the transition that all 11-year-olds have to make when they move from primary school to high school, which for some students can be disturbing, or even traumatic. Most high schools have a structured programme of liaison with 'feeder' primary schools, and induction arrangements for new students, to which this project can very usefully contribute. It may therefore be appropriate that the project takes place towards the end of Year 10 during the summer term: this would give the drama students an opportunity to perform in front of a substantial visiting audience, or for them to visit the feeder primary schools 'on tour'. If undertaken in its entirety, this unit is a substantial piece of work, which could be sustained through 15–20 hours of teaching.

As well as addressing some of the more common uncertainties and concerns that year six pupils might have about their impending move, the final performance can be shaped to focus upon specific issues or procedures common to a particular school.

The structured approach to creating the piece is based upon a detailed sequence of tasks and exercises that provide a coherent framework within which the students can construct their own play. These are included as suggestions, and although they are written in detail and can be followed in that way, it is up to the group and the director or facilitator to decide the direction in which the work should progress. It may be possible to hand ownership of the work solely to the students at a relatively early stage, allowing them the chance to experience acting, technical and directing roles. However, for less experienced or less confident students, we hope that the given structure will provide the balance of challenge and security necessary to stimulate creative responses.

Whichever approach the teacher decides is appropriate for a particular group, the intention is to engage the students in the devising process as quickly as possible, and this is one of the main benefits of this project – its ability to galvanise and motivate a group with the irresistible deadline of a performance in front of an audience.

As reflection and evaluation of both the process and the product now feature in all GCSE drama courses, you may wish to base a piece of coursework upon this project. Suggestions and writing frames are provided in a portfolio style that would allow the students the chance to comment upon their individual contribution as well as the groups' progress as a whole. Encouraging the students to use a rehearsal journal will help them when it comes to writing a final summative response.

Next stop high school **unit map**

Activity	Description	Resources	Teacher notes
Activity 1	'High school' brainstorm; memories of primary school.		
Activity 2	Construct the primary school playground. Thought track 'rumours'. Establish list of primary children's concerns.		
Activity 3	The context of the project. Initial thinking. Framing the drama.		
Activity 4	Pairs improvisations: primary school children the night before . . .		
Activity 5	Opening scene: 'What if . . .' exercise.		
Activity 6	Families: three scenes.		
Activity 7	Establishing the central character. Direct address/figurative mime: toys.		
Activity 8	Pixel: 'magic' remote control.		
Activity 9	Survival guide: school gates. Stock characters. The quest.		
Activity 10	Short scenes: Sam can't cope. Play, pause, rewind. Stylised acting.		
Activity 11	Positive aspects of school: photograph album.		
Activity 12	Final scene: 'Can't wait . . .' lines.		
Activity 13	Performance, workshop and evaluation.	Resource sheets 1, 2, 3 and 4	

Activity 1

In a circle, ask for the students' responses to the words 'high school', written on the board. Ask each student for one word or phrase that they associate with school. Record their responses.

Once everyone has responded, consider the list. What proportion of responses was negative? How many were positive? There will most probably be an imbalance towards negative responses and you might want to spend a few minutes discussing why this might be so. Do the students not agree with the 'best days of your life' theory? It may be necessary to repeat the exercise but this time ask the students to focus on the positive aspects of school life.

Ask the group to consider their memories of primary school. How was it different to their current school? Was it more enjoyable? Why?

Activity 2

Explain that this exercise will introduce a project that the group is going to undertake for the next few weeks. Ask the students to imagine their old primary school playground. What activities are taking place? How are the pupils grouped? Is there a difference between what the boys and the girls are doing? Emphasise that this exercise will demand co-operation with each other as well as the ability to adapt their ideas spontaneously as they join in with the work.

Open out the circle so that there is a large acting area in the middle.

> We are going to create a still image of a primary school playground at lunchtime. We will build up the image in layers, as a montage. As I call out your number, you will take your place in the image. You will have to look carefully at what other people have done and interpret each other's positions and postures before you join in. You are not allowed to talk to each other.

Start calling out the numbers, leaving only a few seconds for each student to find their place in the image.

Once the image is complete and all the students are in place, explain that you are going to use the technique of thought tracking to introduce the theme of the drama work:

> I want you all to think back in time. Try to remember your feelings and thoughts as an 11-year-old, when you were about to start high school. It is the last day of term in your primary school. Tomorrow is the first day of the summer vacation and in September you start high school. If I touch you on the shoulder, and ask you a question, answer in the first person using the word 'I . . .'

- *Are you looking forward to starting high school in September?*
- *What will you miss about your old school?*
- *Have you heard any stories or rumours about your high school?*
- *Are all your friends going to the same school?*
- *Are you nervous about September?*
- *What are you most worried about?*
- *What are you going to take with you on your first day?*
- *What is the worst thing that could happen to you?*
- *What is the best thing that could happen to you?*

Once you have completed the questioning in role, sit the group in a circle and discuss their responses. Draw up a list of the major worries and concerns that primary pupils have about coming up to secondary school. The list might look something like this:

- getting lost in such a large building;
- being bullied by older students;
- difficult homework;
- strict teachers;

- detentions or other punishments;
- exams and work load;
- following complicated timetables and understanding new subjects;
- losing dinner money or bus fare;
- not knowing the answers to difficult questions;
- not making friends, or being split up from friends;
- school buses;
- 'fitting in' to the new environment.

Activity 3

At this stage it will be helpful to provide something of the context for the project:

> Over the next few weeks the whole group will be working together to create a play aimed at primary school children who will be starting high school in September. The play will not simply have to entertain the Year 6 audience – and this will be essential if the play is to be successful – but it will also attempt to inform or educate them. In this way it relates to a style of theatre called theatre in education (TIE) . . .

It is very likely that the group has at some time seen some TIE or other forms of touring theatre as part of their wider school experience, and you may wish to relate the project to examples of good practice with which the group is familiar. They may be aware that 'pure' forms of theatre in education are *participatory* and demand high levels of organisation and skill. Although this project does provide some opportunities for interactive or participatory work with the audience, due to the inevitable time constraints this may be limited in practice. It may be fruitful to use the term 'theatre for young people' as a more accurate description of the finished play.

As well as focusing upon 'educating' and entertaining their audience, a fundamental aspect of the project is in creating a piece of drama for a specific audience – and throughout the developmental and rehearsal process this is to be a major consideration. As the target audience for this project is 10- and 11-year-olds, how will this affect key elements such as style, language, plot, character or the themes explored in the piece? Do the group need to research their audience by meeting them beforehand or making preliminary visits to their school?

It will also be important to develop a policy regarding the play's content, and the particular issues to be explored. Although one intention of the play is presumably to reassure the audience about their first few days in September, is there a risk of propagandising by producing a piece that fails to acknowledge some of the less positive aspects of high school life? How far should the piece 'tell the truth'?

In addition, how far might the choice of content to be explored depend upon its 'treatment'? How far might particular theatrical forms 'allow' difficult material to be dramatised effectively? For instance, would fantasy or comic sequences allow some of the more challenging areas to be explored safely?

A third consideration is the 'angle' or 'frame' chosen to approach the material. 'Frame' refers to the way a drama is focused through the choice of when and where the action is set, the way the action is defined and the selection of key characters. It also relates to the particular focusing questions the playwright (or in this case the devising team) wish to explore. In this drama a number of possible frames might suggest themselves (see Examples 1, 2 and 3).

One frame actually adopted for the play is a 'survival guide' to high school – both literally and figuratively. This frame allows the play to raise the particular, but perhaps unspoken, fears of the audience, and to provide 'counter-scenes' showing the 'reality' of school life. This has proved to be an effective way of striking a balance between 'propaganda' and 'realism'.

Example 1: Looking forward to the event

Who:	A particular primary school student named Sam.
When:	The night before starting secondary school.
Where:	At home.
What:	Sam has nightmares.
Focusing questions:	What is Sam's state of mind? What are her greatest fears? Why is she so anxious? Are her fears based on reality?
Frame for the audience:	Sam's nightmares come to life. Sam is simultaneously 'asleep', and the victim of the stylised nightmares.

Example 2: The event itself

Who:	Sam and Sam's schoolfriends.
When:	The morning of the first day at secondary school.
Where:	The school gates.
What:	The gates are guarded by monsters!
Focusing questions:	Can we establish Sam's character as the 'hero' of the drama, overcoming evil? Can we show Sam's fears as groundless by using exaggeration or parody?
Frame for the audience:	A *quest*. They see the school gates represented as the drawbridge to a gothic castle – establishing a metaphor and style for the play.

Example 3: Looking back on the event

Who:	Sam's form tutor at secondary school.
When:	At the end of the first term.
Where:	In school.
What:	She addresses the audience: 'When Sam first started . . . but now . . .'
Focusing questions:	What did happen to Sam? Did things turn out well in the end? Can we reassure the audience?
Frame for the audience:	A 'documentary' style is established – one of the characters is telling them about what happened to Sam in the past term.

Activity 4

Students might find these simple improvisation tasks useful to further focus their thinking on the concerns of their audience. In groups of four, the students take on the role of primary children meeting in the park for the last time in the summer holidays. What do they discuss? Alternatively, the students sit back to back in pairs. One has telephoned the other, and they have heard something alarming about the first day. Larger groups of five or six might like to create a series of still images to go with each heading from the list of concerns drawn up in the previous discussion.

Activity 5

Explain that the whole group is going to start devising the play by creating the opening scene:

> The first scene of any play is important because it often introduces the key characters and plot elements, and sets the theme and the style of the play. The first scene is also the first opportunity for the actors to focus the audience's attention upon the stage and engage them with the action. I want everyone to think of a line starting with 'What if . . .' that highlights a concern that our audience might have about the first day in September – such as, 'What if I get lost?' or 'What if I get split up from my friends?' You can use some of the ideas from our list.

In the circle, ask students to share their lines. If necessary, write them down.

> How can we use those lines in an interesting, dramatic way on stage that uses the whole group and immediately focuses the audience's attention?

Allow the group to respond to this challenge or experiment with the following ideas:

- The whole group stands in the performance area. The first person to speak has a sports or school bag. When they have said their line they throw the bag to someone else who says their line and so on. Once the last line is said, the whole group shouts 'What if . . .'
- Remind the students of the previous exercise when they built up a still image in layers. This could be effectively used here with each of the group walking on to stage, taking their position in the image and saying their line. At the final 'What if . . .' the image of the playground bursts into life and activity.
- Starting with the still image of the playground, bursts of movement and activity are contrasted with moments of stillness as individuals say their 'What if . . .' lines.
- Students might wish to use music or create a song, rap, poem or rhythmical response based on the 'What if . . .' lines that could effectively introduce the play's theme.

Once the group has explored different ideas and has 'sketched in' the opening scene, they can progress to the next section.

Activity 6

Referring back to the list that the pupils drew up in Activity 3, are the expectations of parents or other family members mentioned? If the students have any older brothers or sisters, what advice did they give about how to cope with the first day? What advice did their parents or other members of the family give them? Was this good advice? Knowing what they know now, what advice would they give to their own children? In groups of four or five, ask the students to improvise a short scene that shows a 'typical' family. In each family there is one boy or girl who is starting school the next day.

Suggest to the group that the families – and the advice they give – should be contrasting. For instance:

- The first could be a family indifferent to what is to happen the next day and which gives all the wrong sort of advice: 'Ask your father', 'I'm busy', 'Just don't be rude to your teachers', or 'If you need a pen, borrow one.'
- The second family might be the opposite, and put unrealistically high expectations upon the boy or girl: 'You must get to the top of the class immediately', 'Answer all the questions the teachers ask', or 'Your brother won the school prize for brains – that's what we expect from you' or 'You must enrol in all of the extra-curricular activities.'
- In the third family the parents try to be supportive and encouraging without putting too much pressure on the boy or girl: 'Just do your best, that's all anyone can ask of you', or 'If you need help, ask one of the teachers.'

In these scenes students can explore the use of exaggeration and stylisation to create humour. The students might make the first and second families as humorous as possible by presenting the characters as exaggerated, cartoon-like stereotypes. The third family could be more 'realistic' to contrast with these stylised characters. If all the families are on stage and the action follows immediately one from the other, encourage some continuity of the scenes by having each one ending the same way, perhaps with a repeated line of dialogue or an action. Encourage the improvisations to be brief – a maximum of two minutes in length.

Once the groups have had the chance to prepare their work, share the scenes by performing one after the other. Do they contrast enough with each other? Are they entertaining and engaging?

Activity 7

It is time now to introduce a central character to be the focus of the play's action. Ask the students to choose a name for the character that could be male or female, for example Alex, Tony or Sam. The idea of sharing the role – so that more than one actor portrays the same character – symbolises the 'universal' nature of the character and would allow different actors the opportunity of playing one of the central characters throughout the play. Ask the group to consider ways that this convention could be made clear to the audience, perhaps by using an exaggerated piece of costume, or a prop like a school bag or tie that is identified with this character.

Explain that this scene follows on directly from the 'families' scene, and introduces Sam, who is the boy or girl from the third family, due to start school tomorrow. Sam goes to her bedroom to get an early night for the big day tomorrow. After saying a few words using *direct address* to the audience and introducing herself, Sam falls asleep. In her room there is a real or prop television, and she is surrounded by typical toys and posters found in any 11-year-old's room. These are to be portrayed in *figurative mime* by the rest of the group.

It may be worth discussing with the group the subtle change in audience/performer relationship that occurs here through the convention of direct address. When Sam speaks directly to the audience in this way, how does the play change for them?

- Will the audience expect this to happen? Will the convention be familiar to them – can the class think of other kinds of drama where this happens that students of this age might have seen?
- How does this device make the drama different from, say, a TV soap opera?
- By acknowledging that the audience is present in this way the 'frame' of the drama changes from 'we are eavesdropping on someone else's life' to 'someone is showing and telling us something that happened to them'. Why might this be a good way of approaching a project like 'Next stop . . . high school'?

In a similar way the use of figurative mime to portray the toys in the bedroom establishes a particular style for the drama.

- How might the audience respond to this technique?
- What does it say about the play? It clearly reinforces the non-naturalistic nature of the work; how might this change the way the audience 'receives' the drama? Does performing it in this style make it less 'real' for them? In what sense – are they likely to take it less seriously?

As Sam falls asleep, the previously frozen toys and posters assume a life of their own and start to torment and tease her. Sam wakes with a start and decides to turn on the television to help her get to sleep. This is when she meets the other central character who will act as guide and mentor through the rest of the play.

Depending on the group size and how you wish to work, it is possible to approach this section in a number of ways. You can divide up the tasks between the students and work as a whole group, or have individual groups prepare the nightmare toys, share the work and then choose the best ideas.

It is relatively straightforward to set up a video camera on a tripod offstage that is linked to a television on stage by an audio-visual cable. As long as the actor offstage can hear the actor on stage, it creates the illusion of Sam being able to 'talk to' the television. Alternatively, a frame of some sort or pool of light can represent the television screen.

Choose the actor who is going to play the first Sam; this, logically, is the son or daughter from the 'normal' family of the previous scene. Ask him or her to improvise a short opening speech to the audience using direct address, introducing who they are:

Hi, I'm Sam. I'm starting at the high school tomorrow. To tell you the truth, I'm a bit nervous . . .

Ask the other students to take up position as the inanimate toys and objects in Sam's room. They need to improvise what happens when they come alive and torment Sam. As the group works on this improvisation, encourage them to think of design elements that would support the action.

- *How might lighting be used to indicate a darkened bedroom and to signify that Sam is asleep?*
- *How could music or sound effects help build up tension and atmosphere?*

Activity 8

As Sam awakes from her nightmare, the toys are motionless again and back in their original positions. Sam decides to switch on the television to try and take her mind off worrying. As she scans through the channels *Pixel* appears on the screen. This character is to be Sam's mentor and guide, and is the vehicle for reinforcing key learning points for the audience.

The students portraying Sam and Pixel will now have to improvise the dialogue between a very surprised Sam, and Pixel. They should introduce the idea that Pixel can help Sam overcome her fears, perhaps by using a device such as a 'magic' remote control that can pause and rewind the action on stage. But first the students must solve a technical problem: Pixel must get out of the television – or Sam must get *into* the television. Encourage them to experiment with interesting ways to 'move' from one 'world' to another.

Activity 9

Ask the actors playing Pixel and Sam to devise a short section of dialogue that will get them to the first part of the *survival guide* titled 'the school gates'. Then, brief the rest of the group:

> *Although we want to make our play as entertaining as possible, one of our aims is to help inform them. To help us do this we are going to develop a 'survival guide' to high school. By using this device we can show scenes based upon things going wrong, and then, using Pixel's remote control, we can stop and rewind the action and show the right way of doing things. In this section, we are going to create the first obstacle for Sam to overcome, the dreaded school gates. For Sam, what might the school gates represent? How can we create the idea of an imposing barrier, just by using our bodies?*

Once the students have created the school gates, they have to interact with Sam when she approaches them, not letting her pass. There is potential here for a number of characters to be played by the actors who form the gate. For instance, a pair of gatekeepers could peer over the top of the gate, asking impossible riddles. Other possibilities:

- gargoyles who do not like Sam because she is too clean and smart;
- 'caretakers' who do not want Sam to come in and mess up their orderly school;
- a group of fiendish teachers who do not want the school to be disrupted by pupils: 'It runs like clockwork with no kids cluttering up the place.'

In this section of the drama students might base their characterisations on 'stock characters' that are instantly recognisable and rely on cultural *types* or *stereotypes* for their personality and physical characteristics. Deriving originally from Greek and Roman theatre, students may be familiar with the use of stock characters in Comedia del'Arte, Shakespeare and in many more contemporary forms of theatre as well as film and television drama.

The following list of stock characters might serve as a starting point for students' own investigations:

- *The Hero*
- *The Villain*
- *The Guide or Mentor*
- *The Damsel in Distress*

- *The Clown*
- *The Mad Scientist*
- *The Assistant or Sidekick*
- *The Vamp or Femme Fatale*

Ask the students to list examples of these various types of stock character in stories, plays or films with which they are familiar. Could any of the characters in Next stop . . . high school conform to these recognisable stock types? How might the use of stock characters in this way help their audience to engage with the play?

As this section of the drama is structured in the form of a *quest* students may also be able to make suggestions based upon their knowledge of similar structures used in stories, films and computer games. (Examples from literature might be *The Holy Grail*, *The Lord of the Rings* or *The Golden Fleece*.) In such a quest, as in Sam's adventures in the drama, the hero must acquire artefacts or knowledge and overcome a range of villains in order to achieve success and prove their heroism.

Sam goes back to Pixel, who has been watching from the side. Pixel then sets the record straight: 'Everything is scary first time round, but remember the school is *your* school. It belongs to the pupils. Without you, the school would not exist. So go back and tell that to the gates in your loudest voice.'

We then see Sam challenging the gates – and the gates subsequently opening. As the work on the scene progresses, encourage the group to consider how they could reinforce the learning point for the audience. For example, students could design a placard that emphasises the message, and involve them in reciting it as a chant or spell.

Activity 10

Explain to the group that the next phase of the work is going to cover some other important 'learning areas' for the audience. Referring back to the list of 'worries and concerns' created in Activity 3, individual groups can now create a series of short scenes that show Sam tackling different situations.

In each situation, we see Sam not being able to cope. Pixel then stops the action with her pause button, tells Sam where she has gone wrong – and what she should have done – and then replays the situation again, this time with Sam following the advice and getting it 'right'.

This convention of *play*, *pause* and *rewind* allows each point to be made clear for the audience. It also provides opportunities for audience interaction as different characters freeze the action and ask the audience's advice as to the best course of action.

Each of these improvisations should have a specific and clear learning point relevant to the audience. There might be specific information about a particular school – 'If you get lost, ask a prefect, they wear red jumpers', or more general points: 'Making friends will happen but it can take time', or 'Don't be afraid to ask for help'. Throughout the scenes it is important for the actor playing Pixel to emphasise the point that this is a journey through Sam's imagination, and that all the situations are exaggerated images of what she thinks school is like, based on rumours and stories she has heard.

The following scenarios can be used as a basis for scenes exploring some of the usual concerns and worries of primary school pupils. The 'linking' characters between all of these scenes will be Sam and Pixel. The character of Sam can continue to be played by different actors, but it might be more difficult to adopt this approach with the Pixel 'mentor' or 'guide' character. The actor taking this role will also have to liaise with all the different groups preparing scenes.

As these scenes represent Sam's imagination, the style of acting of the characters Sam encounters might reflect this. It may be fruitful to experiment with different methods of stylisation; slow motion, exaggerated gestures or vocal effects might all be fruitfully explored. There are also decisions to be made regarding props and costumes. It is possible to present this work very effectively with no costumes and using mime to represent props. However, you may wish to consider constructing some props that emphasise the style of the piece and help to convey the surreal nature of Sam's journey.

As this is the section when the students can really take control of the scenes that are to be included in the play, it may be appropriate at this stage to clarify the content that the piece is to cover. Weightier issues such as bullying need careful planning and consideration if they are not to reinforce preconceptions and fears. The students should bear in mind the age and the 'needs' of the audience during all their devising work.

Don't panic!

Sam passes through the school gates and wanders into the school. She encounters a group of panicking newly arrived Year 7 pupils who are acting as if they are lost in a dangerous jungle rather than a school. As soon as Sam arrives she too starts to panic, until Pixel steps in, pauses the action and gives the advice: 'First – don't panic. If you get lost use your map, planner or diary.'

Pixel produces a large map that she gives to Sam. The panicky pupils calm down, see where they are supposed to go and leave, taking the map with them.

Could you repeat that please?

Sam goes wandering off again, this time bumping into a group of 'cartoon' school caretakers. They are attempting to fix something, polish a floor or change a light bulb using an enormous manual. One reads out very complicated instructions, another repeats them in a shorter version while yet another actually attempts the task:

'Right, "Changing a light bulb in 32 easy steps. Step one – remove offending, non-functioning, luminescent sphere."'
'You what?'
'He means take out the old bulb.'
'Oh, right.'

After we see the caretakers undertaking this very difficult task, Sam asks them the way to her form or tutor room. They give her extremely long-winded and ridiculously detailed directions. Sam patently does not understand them but thanks them and heads off on her way, obviously confused. Pixel steps in with the advice 'If you don't understand something, then say so.'

Sam returns to the caretakers and asks them to repeat their instructions. This time their directions are clear and understandable.

You girl, what are you doing?

Sam encounters a group of fiendish teachers who are walking down the corridor. We hear them discussing all the punishments they have given out, how much homework they are going to set, what they do to students who are late. When they bump into Sam they start inspecting her as if she was a soldier on parade.

Pixel steps in to pause the action. 'Your imagination is working overtime again. Teachers aren't like this. They are there to help you and want you to settle in as quickly as possible. So don't be afraid of them, just be polite and be yourself.'

First day exams

As Sam is about to reach her form room, a group of Year 7 pupils form a line with chairs in front of her. Following the instructions of the teacher, they sit and Sam is challenged as to where her chair is; 'Don't you know it is first day exams? Sit down child.'

The exams start and are ridiculously hard. There are only 30 seconds to complete each paper; all the pupils mime writing furiously before the papers are collected in. The pace is frantic and frenetic until Pixel pauses the action. 'You don't get a test on your first day. Sure, there are exams at different times in the year, but you'll have time and help to prepare for them. This is just your imagination working overtime.'

A friend for life

Sam next raises her concerns about being split up from her friends and her fear of not making new friends. Pixel decides to show Sam that making friends is easy and introduces her to a Professor (of 'Friendshipology'?).

The professor tells Sam that by using the very latest technology, 'making' friends is no problem. In the laboratory a line of frozen students make up the different models available. There are lots to choose from and we see a selection from the 'sports model', 'foreign exchange student' and 'competitive model'. At the flick of a switch each comes to life for a moment, but, of course, none is suitable. The 'rich model' looks down her nose at Sam, the 'fashionable model' is too vain, and Sam gets upset.

Pixel arrives, saying that this was just an example to show that friends cannot be 'manufactured'. 'Don't worry! Just be yourself and try to get on with people. You'll soon find out who you get on best with and they will become your friends.'

Pixel could point out a couple of characters playing together or swapping cards or stories and encourage Sam to go over and join in as an example of how to start making friends.

Don't you know anything?

As the 'friendship' scene ends Sam is swept up by a group of pupils all heading towards their first lesson.

Once inside the classroom, Sam goes through a terrible experience. The teacher keeps asking impossible questions that everyone else can answer apart from Sam. Even worse, when the teacher asks if anyone does not understand, Sam is the only one to put up her hand.

Pixel steps in to stop the action again, reminding Sam that this is what she is imagining lessons will be like. 'Remember, everyone is in the same boat. There might be times when you don't know the answers to questions, but that is why you are in school . . . to learn. As long as you do your best, that's all anyone can ask of you.'

Activity 11

The previous scenes will make up the bulk of the play and will take some time to prepare. As the students shape and refine their work, encourage them to consider how the scenes will link to each other. Can they think of ways that will help maintain the continuity of the play, perhaps through the use of lighting, sound or music? Again, they may wish to use slides, placards or displays that signal the scenes' titles or learning points.

In this scene we are going to show all the positive things that Sam can achieve in her five years at this school. Pixel is going to show Sam a photograph album made up of images from her future school life. As she does, in small groups we are going to create still images, so the photo album comes alive for the audience. The pictures should reflect the fact that school is not just about exams and doing well academically. It is also about taking part in all sorts of things; learning a musical instrument, acting in the school play, running the 100 metres for sports day, going on a trip or residential, or the school leavers' party or prom. All of these things are parts of school life.

Allow the group some time to prepare these images. The emphasis should be on creating dynamic, exciting pictures that can be presented to Sam and the audience in an awards ceremony or retrospective *This Is Your Life* style. They should represent the opportunities for high school students beyond the classroom. Having Sam take her place in each image, or developing each photograph with 30 seconds of speech and action, can extend the scene.

Activity 12

Explain that the group now needs to consider the final scene of the play. A suggestion could be that Sam is back in her room, surrounded by the toys from the earlier 'nightmare' scene. As she wakes up for her first day of high school, she looks for Pixel on the television, but there is no one there. Was it all a dream? Sam is keen to get going, is ready for anything, and remembers all the advice she has been given. As a whole group the students could compose the final speech, which should include the key learning points of the scenes.

Once Sam has delivered her speech and left the bedroom we could finish off the play as a whole group. Remember the first scene and your 'What if . . .' lines? You are going to compose another line, this time starting with 'Can't wait . . .' which highlights a positive aspect of school, like 'Can't wait to make new friends', 'Can't wait to learn French' or 'Can't wait to go on the different trips'. What might make a suitable 'finale' for our drama? What would be a good final line? 'Can't wait to see you all here' or 'Can't wait for September', perhaps?

Activity 13

Performance, workshop and evaluation

At the end of the performance you may wish to consider allowing the audience the opportunity to talk to the actors or ask questions. This is simply achieved by inviting the cast to sit in the performance space at the end of the piece and conducting a question and answer session, but will need planning. Very often the audience will want to know first hand about the experiences of the members of the group as well as clearing up any points they missed or found confusing from the play. The audience may also wish to find out about how the play has been devised.

Alternatively, a more explicitly theatrical workshop can be constructed using a range of dramatic techniques with which the students may be familiar from their own drama lessons. A simple workshop can be developed by extending the question and answer session into hotseating particular characters, or by re-enacting scenes from the play – perhaps with a member of the audience as Sam.

Prior to the performance the group may elect to create supporting materials – perhaps a programme or handout. It might reinforce points that have been made in the play and could include cartoons or drawings as well as text. This task provides a particularly good context for the use of ICT design and publishing software. Students might also consider composing a feedback sheet for the audience, which can be completed and returned later.

As part of the work your students undertake you may wish to make use of the evaluation sheets provided (Resource sheets 1–3). Once copied, students can use them as the framework for a range of evaluative work. Alternatively, a structure for a piece of reflective writing based on the project is provided (Resource sheet 4), and this may be helpful for teachers keen to encourage a more discursive evaluation of the work.

NEXT STOP . . . HIGH SCHOOL

Resource sheet 1

Name	*Next stop . . . high school* portfolio

Write a list of all the things we think Year 6 will be worried about.

_____

_____

_____

_____

_____

_____

Describe your first day at high school. Include details about your feelings and what actually happened. Was it how you expected it to be? Where there any surprises? Be as detailed as you can.

_____

_____

_____

_____

_____

_____

Write an imaginary diary account from the point of view of the character starting high school. It is the night before the first day of term. Describe how they are feeling and what they are looking forward to or are concerned about.

_____

_____

_____

_____

_____

_____

Write a list of words you think describes how Year 6 might be feeling.

_____

_____

_____

_____

_____

On a separate A4 sheet of paper, design a leaflet to be given to the Year 6 pupils when they arrive for the performance. The leaflet should include advice and guidance about coping with the move to high school. Try to be as imaginative as possible, use images, cartoons and pictures to help make your points clear. The leaflet should reflect the learning points made in your performance.

NEXT STOP . . . HIGH SCHOOL

Resource sheet 2

Name	*Next stop . . . high school* portfolio

Describe in detail what your play was aiming to achieve. Who was the target audience? What do you understand by the phrase 'theatre in education'?

_____

_____

_____

_____

_____

_____

Write a list of the scenes that were included in the final performance. Briefly describe what each scene was about.

_____

_____

_____

_____

_____

_____

How did the age of the audience affect the choice of language, scenes and overall style of the play?

_____

_____

_____

_____

_____

_____

Describe the way that you devised the play. Was this an effective way of working?

_____

_____

_____

_____

_____

NEXT STOP . . . HIGH SCHOOL

Resource sheet 3

Name	*Next stop . . . high school* portfolio

Describe what you have contributed to the success of the performance. What have you added to the ideas in the scenes during rehearsals?

_____

_____

_____

_____

_____

_____

Describe a character that you portrayed. Describe how you changed your voice, movement and gesture to suit the role. Evaluate how effective this was when you performed.

_____

_____

_____

_____

_____

_____

Do you feel that the play got the important messages over to the audience? Choose a scene that you felt worked the best in performance. Why was it so good? Was the scene's message clear at all times?

_____

_____

_____

_____

_____

_____

On separate paper, write a new scene to include in your play. Choose what the scene is about – what message is it trying to get across to the audience? Make this aim very clear. Include stage directions in brackets, the names of the characters on one side, and their dialogue. Your scene should be about a page long.

NEXT STOP . . . HIGH SCHOOL

Resource sheet 4

Essay title 'Next stop . . . high school' – evaluation

1 Opening paragraph

Explain what the project was about – *creating a piece of theatre called 'Next stop . . . high school'. This was a piece of theatre in education aimed at reassuring Year 6 pupils about coming up to high school.* Explain that the whole group devised the play over several weeks, working on different scenes sometimes in small groups and sometimes as a whole group. Explain that the play contained serious messages within the scenes that the audience could learn from – *we wanted to educate and entertain our audience.*

2 Write a brief summary of the different scenes that were included in the final performance and the messages contained in each scene

3 In this section you will describe and evaluate the devising process.

Explain how the scenes were devised – *We discussed what the scenes would be about and then improvised around the themes in small groups. Then we would show the work and decide which sections we would keep. Sometimes we worked as a whole group devising the scenes.* Give an example of a scene from each way of working. Which was the best way of working, as a whole group or in smaller groups? Why do you think this was a good way of working?

What ideas did you contribute? Give some examples of scenes that you helped to shape.

Your audience was very young. Describe how you had to think of your audience's reaction and what you hoped to achieve – to educate and entertain: *We had to keep language very simple and make the plot very easy to follow.* How did you make it easy for the audience to understand what was going on? How did you emphasise certain key points?

4 In this section you will describe and evaluate the performance

Comment on your personal thoughts about the success of the performance: Did you feel the performances went well? Why did it go well? – *The audience seemed to enjoy the performances; they listened to all the important speeches. At the end of the performance, they asked questions that showed they had been listening and paying attention.*

Comment on how you used lighting, music, sound or technical effects like the television and the camera (if your group used them). Did these all help the overall performance? How did they help? Are there any technical aspects that could have worked better? What would you do differently next time?

5 Conclusion – in this section you will be evaluating your contribution to the performance

Describe what role or roles you had in the play. How did you change your voice, body and movement to act out this part? Was your acting clear to the audience? Did you remember your lines and your cues? Did you stay in role and concentrate? What did you find hard about performing? – *I was nervous, and I had a lot to remember, but I managed to stay in role and say my lines loudly and clearly.* What did you enjoy the most about performing?

Choose someone else in the play that you thought acted very well. Why did you think they were very good? Describe what they did.

6 Write a new scene to insert into your play

Choose what the scene is about – what message is it trying to get across to the audience? Make this aim very clear. Now write out your scene like this example below. It includes stage directions in brackets, the names of the characters on one side and their lines. Your scene should be about a page long.

Scene title: Sam gets organised. Aim: to show the audience how to use their homework diaries

(On stage a single light picks out Sam who is sitting on a chair holding a pile of books. She looks worried. Pixel appears next to her.)

PIXEL:	What's wrong Sam? You look so sad.
SAM:	Look, the teachers have given me all this homework to finish, I'm not sure where to begin.
PIXEL:	Okay, lets get some help. I'll call my friend, 'Organiser'. *(He fiddles with his remote control and suddenly 'Organiser' appears on stage. He has an massive homework diary in his hands.)*
ORGANISER:	Here I am, I'll help you get organised. Now let's see . . . *(He turns over the pages in his book.)*

The scene carries on as 'Organiser' helps Sam.

Lilliput

Introduction and context

This work was originally developed from a series of workshops that explored conflict resolution between young people caught up in the ongoing conflict in Northern Ireland. By approaching such a sensitive topic in an indirect way, the students were able to bring their own unique experiences of conflict into a more public domain and were able to begin to challenge their own prejudices and discriminations.

Even though this unit explores some serious themes, the activities and tasks are fun and light-hearted. There is an opportunity to explore satire and parody, and implicit in that is the chance for the students to create some comedic and larger than life characters. The drama also explores the way a piece of fictional writing, in this case Jonathan Swift's *Gulliver's Travels*, can be used as a stimulus for drama.

We anticipate that a group exploring all the activities in this unit would take about five one-hour lessons to complete the tasks.

Activity 1

Hand out the 'eyewitness accounts' (Resource sheet 1, page 109) that are taken from Swift's *Gulliver*. Explain to the group that travellers to a mysterious land brought these accounts back. The students' task is to use this evidence to investigate and reconstruct their impressions of what life might be like in this strange society.

Ask the students to read the accounts in groups of four or five. It may be appropriate to structure this exercise so that each group interprets only one of the accounts; these can then be shared and discussed with the whole class.

Once the class has had the opportunity to explore the written accounts, their next task is to imagine that, along with the eyewitness descriptions they have just read, some fragments of film footage were also discovered. Explain that, unfortunately, these short pieces of film were corrupted in some way and that the accompanying soundtrack has been lost. The groups' task is to recreate these moments of 'archive film' showing aspects of life in this strange land. Although there is no soundtrack and the actors cannot use dialogue, the group is able to add their own narrative links.

This is a good point for the group to begin to explore the idea of satire and parody. You may wish to offer a definition:

> *Satire: A literary form which attacks human vice or folly through irony, derision or wit. Satire often takes the easily identifiable elements of something and exaggerates or heightens them to make a humorous point.*

Ask the group to list any television wildlife or history documentaries with which they might be familiar. What elements are common to these sorts of programmes? As each group prepares a short extract of the 'discovered film' to perform to the rest of the group can they use any of these programmes' identifiable features?

Lilliput unit map

Activity	Description	Resources	Teacher notes
Activity 1	Eyewitness accounts; recreated archive film footage.	Resource sheet 1	
Activity 2	The cut finger incident: dramatisation; repercussions.	Resource sheet 2	
Activity 3	Big and Little-endians: rumours; graffiti wall.	Pens, paper	
Activity 4	Three concepts; propaganda films.		
Activity 5	Peace conference; card roles.	Playing cards	
Activity 6	Lilliput 100 years in the future.		
Activity 7	Reflection: contemporary, historical or literary examples of secret weapons.		

> _. . . and here we see for the first time, the quaint custom that is the way that these strange people select their leaders . . ._

Once all the work has been shared, ask the students to summarise what they infer about this society:

- What does the group think of the people that live there?
- What might everyday life in such a place be like?
- How does it contrast with our own society; how might it be similar?

Activity 2

Inform the students that in spite of these peoples' intriguing customs and seemingly happy existence, evidence has come to light that all was not well in their society: there was evidence of conflict and civil war.

Keeping the students in their same working groups, read or visually present Resource sheet 2 (page 110) – a newly discovered 'eyewitness' account of life in this land. In discussion, make sure that the students understand fully the implications and severity of the described war. Explain that in order to understand the feelings of the people caught up in this conflict, each group will re-enact the seemingly innocent starting point – the incident of the cut finger which sparks off the fighting – in as much detail as possible.

Clearly there is potential for comedy here, but remind the group that playing such a seemingly absurd incident in a totally serious manner will probably be more effective than playing the scene for laughs. The satire lies in the way such a trivial incident is treated with utter seriousness by the characters involved.

After sharing some of these performances, explain that the groups will now be focusing upon the repercussions of the cut finger incident. Returning to the text, ask each group to imagine one incident that happened as a consequence arising from the royal cut finger. As an analogy to make this clearer, the students could imagine a pebble thrown into a pond. The pebble represents the accident with the egg, and each ripple radiating out is a consequence that ends in a civil war costing the lives of thousands of people. As the groups consider these incidents, they should imagine incidents that vary in seriousness from the trivial to the momentous.

Once the groups have finished devising, arrange the room with a chair and table or block in the centre of the space. A neatly arranged egg cup and napkin serve effectively as a visual cue and represent the moment the incident happened and its triviality. Now ask the groups to arrange themselves so that they radiate out from the table – the further away from the centre they are, the 'further' away – in terms of time, geographical distance and significance – is the incident they are enacting.

Positioning the groups may take some negotiation. Explain to them that they will perform their work as a sequence which represents the period of the six rebellions referred to in the account.

To trigger this performance sequence, sit in the chair as teacher in role and re-enact some elements of one of the earlier dramas based on the cut finger incident that have just been presented by the group. You may have to agree this sequence with the class. Each group can then take their cue from the group preceding it as the dramas radiate out towards the edge of the room, presenting incidents growing in seriousness and importance as they go.

Activity 3

The following sequence of activities is designed to explore the rival 'Big-endian' and 'Little-endian' cultures within Lilliput that arose following the cut finger incident. As the work progresses, the students might start to identify parallels with modern society in relation to racial stereotyping, religious intolerance and xenophobia.

Divide the class into two groups and give each one their group name and identity – the Little-endians and the Big-endians. Separate the groups by moving them to opposite ends of the classroom.

Within their newly assigned groups, ask each student to find a partner. In role as either a Big- or a Little-endian, ask each pair to share gossip, rumour or myths told about the rival group. Encourage imaginative and outlandish accusations or slurs; perhaps some students might invent a purely fictitious incident or action which casts the other group in a negative light. After a few minutes and once the pairs have had time to invent and share their rumours and gossip, invite them to join with other pairs to share and spread their inventions. Once these fours have shared all their stories, they could join into eights and then into 16s – by this time the rumours and stereotypes are well on the way to becoming part of the groups' 'folklore' and belief system. If this large group work is impractical, simply share some of the work by asking individuals to say what they had heard from their partner.

Lay out some large rolls of newsprint or pieces of sugar paper with pens enough for each of the two groups to transfer the rumours and stories they have heard about the other side onto paper – in the form of graffiti. Explain that, once complete, the 'graffiti walls' will be stuck on the classroom wall to 'mark the territory' of the two groups and symbolise the boundary between them.

Once the graffiti walls are complete, ask each of the two rival groups to form a large tableau in front of 'their' wall. The image should symbolise their feelings of belonging – and their attitude to outsiders.

This idea of walls and boundaries can provoke further thought as to how different societies use physical divides to separate groups in conflict. Can the students identify any real examples from history or the present day?

As a means of encouraging the students to reflect upon the exercise, ask each group to swap positions and take a trip into 'enemy territory'. This will enable them to read the scurrilous (and of course untrue) things written about them by the other side.

- What does this activity tell us about the two rival cultures?
- What does it tell us of the way that 'tribes' of this sort behave?
- Can the group suggest any 'real-life' parallels (rival football teams, schools, towns or cities, perhaps even religious or cultural groupings)?

Activity 4

Following this reflective discussion, and to add another layer of understanding to the drama, it may be helpful at this point to introduce three recognised concepts which are useful in understanding the processes which drive conflict and reconciliation. Of course, these ideas may be challenging for some age groups to grasp. You may wish to simplify some of the more difficult concepts in order to help the students understand that there are significant forces that influence how we make decisions about groups of people. These are:

Deification: Deification is the process through which people elevate others to the status of gods. An example of this might be the way in which Princess Diana was regarded after her death – or the way that certain pop stars or sports personalities are 'worshipped'.

Reification: Reification refers to the way in which people, ideas or concepts can be treated as concrete things – and can be regarded as material 'objects' to be classified and described. An example of this might be the way in which categories of people – 'yuppies' or 'hooligans', for instance – are created with little regard for the individuals themselves. Reification is a key tool in war propaganda, as whole countries or races can be categorised into groups that are then easy to present negatively. The de-humanising element of this process is recognised as being a key concept to recruit and encourage soldiers to fight. The individual human life is taken out of the equation and replaced by a 'type' or category of person.

Idealisation: Idealisation describes the portrayal of things or people in an ideal form or character. Negative aspects are left to one side as the person or thing is presented in their 'best light'. Politicians are often guilty of this when applying 'spin' to a new policy or initiative. During times of war, governments and leaders might invest much effort in presenting an idealised version of life in their country or society, a life that is under threat from the enemy.

Once these concepts have been discussed, divide the Big-endians and the Little-endians into groups of four or five. Explain that, due to the ensuing civil war, the Ministry for Information in both groups has asked for submissions of scenes suitable to be included in a propaganda film. The film is designed to promote their particular cultural group and devalue their rival's way of life. These short dramas should illustrate one of the three concepts described above. For instance, scenes might show the deification of leaders or 'heroes' from the war, the idealisation of life in their own society, or the reification of the opposing 'tribe'.

Some guidance or explanation of propaganda and how it can be used might be appropriate. Posters and literature from all the combatants in World War I and II are excellent and accessible examples of effective propaganda.

- *What is propaganda designed to do?*
- *What is 'effective' propaganda?*
- *What effect might propaganda have on an audience (a) of members of the same group; (b) of members of the opposing group; (c) of people who are not attached to any particular group?*

As soon as all the students understand their brief, allow each group time to prepare their short submissions. Once created, the work should be presented formally and with a heightened sense of importance as '*this is another tool or weapon that could turn the tide of the war . . .*'

As each group shares its work, ask the audience members to reflect upon their feelings regarding how their cultural group is portrayed. Is there a sense of national pride or patriotism as they watch their particular group idealised? Is there a sense of anger or dismay if they see their way of life pilloried or cheapened?

Once all the work has been presented, discuss the drama work so far:

- *Can you think of recent real-life conflicts which seem similar to the Big-endians' and Little-endians' situation?*
- *Is the use of an analogy or parallel situation effective in the drama? Why?*
- *How important is propaganda in influencing a group's opinion or beliefs?*
- *Are you familiar with any examples of satirical television, drama or film? How does that satire work?*

Activity 5

The final section of the drama focuses on the problems of conflict resolution, and takes the form of a 'peace conference'. To start this section of the work, the teacher narrates a link:

> *The war raged for many years, and many died. Over time, some people even forgot why they were fighting. No family was left unaffected, and each had their own tale of loss to tell. The people hoped that change might come. Eventually, realising the futility of the war, both sides sat down together to try to make peace . . .*

Ask the group to take their places in a circle, alternatively seated Big- and Little-endian. In role as the convenor of the peace conference, explain that the task of the assembled delegates from both sides is to try to draw up a treaty to which both sides can agree, and which will bring peace to the land. Stress the fragile nature of the current truce and praise the delegates for their diplomatic skills and earnest belief in the peace process.

> *Now, is there a representative from the Big-endians and the Little-endians who would start the proceedings by standing and making an opening statement about what they hope this meeting will achieve?*

Once the opening statements have been made, allow the debate to continue, acting as 'chair' for as long as is necessary. To facilitate a more lively discussion, encourage the two sides to consider some of the more difficult questions about reconciliation:

- What about any land or property that is disputed; how will the groups decide who owns what?
- What about compensation for victims of the war?
- How will the war be historically recorded and taught in schools?
- Will any blame be attached to either group as to who started the conflict, or for any atrocities carried out in the name of war?

Stop the meeting and, out of role, ask the students to consider whether peace between the two sides will ever be achieved in this way? If discussion is not enough, what must happen before agreement might be found?

In order to help the students explore the depth of feelings that the delegates might have, place a playing card face down on the floor in front of each student. The group may be familiar with the use of cards in drama; to delineate status, for instance. Explain that in this exercise, the cards will denote the strength of an individual's feelings about their own 'side' and the degree of their radicalism towards the conflict and the other group. For example, a Big-endian drawing a picture card like a jack or a queen will have very strong beliefs and may be dogmatic and extremely unwilling to accept the Little-endians' point of view. On the other hand, a Little-endian drawing a three or a two will be very 'liberal' and, although quite loyal to his or her own side, will be willing to compromise for the sake of a lasting peace.

Once you have explained the rules, allow the students to pick up their cards. They must not share their card with anyone else. Allow a minute's thinking time so that each student can gauge their character's depth of feeling towards the reconciliation and peace process.

To mark their role's changed perspective, ask the students to find a different seat to sit in and then reconvene the conference, letting the discussion run for an appropriate time, before stopping to reflect:

- Is peace any nearer?
- What is getting in the way of the 'peace process'?
- Are particular individuals responsible for holding up the process?
- What suggestions could the group offer to make peace more likely?

At a given signal, ask the students to reveal their cards.

- What does this drama suggest about peace and reconciliation?
- How hard was it for the members of the group who suddenly had to adopt a very different point of view? What does this tell us about how difficult it may be to change people's minds after years of real conflict and hatred?
- Can the group think of a similar peace process that has happened in the past or is happening now?
- Do the events in the drama reflect any elements of these real life situations?

Activity 6

As a final exercise, ask the students to form groups of four. Their task is to imaginatively project a further 100 years into the Lilliputians' future in order to speculate what might have happened after the first peace meeting. Ask the groups to create an extract from a news programme commissioned as part of the centenary anniversary of the first historic peace conference. Some questions that might be answered through their broadcast might be:

- *Does the war still rage on?*
- *Do the two groups still exist or have there been further divisions?*
- *Do people still define themselves by their Big- or Little-endian identity?*
- *Have the people forgotten the original source of the conflict?*
- *Is there any difference between the attitudes of the young and older people?*
- *Are there any stories of hope or triumph over adversity?*

After allowing sufficient preparation time, ask each group to share their short extract. Are there any similarities between the groups? Have the same conclusions been drawn? Is there a feeling of appeasement, or has the group decided that the Big- and Little-endians have never been able to reconcile their differences?

At this point, invite reflective discussion. Can the group suggest ways that may have helped the peace process if it failed, or quickened its resolution if it was successful? For instance:

- a programme of exchanges between Big- and Little-endians, allowing people to swap places for a short time;
- a festival celebrating the differences and similarities between the two cultures;
- an education scheme in schools aimed at re-educating youngsters and removing prejudice;
- integrated cities, suburbs, schools and colleges;
- peace workers and centres whose mission is to bring together both cultures;
- an annual event or ceremony marking the reconciliation of the two sides.

Activity 7

In Jonathan Swift's *Gulliver's Travels*, the war escalates to such a degree that the neighbouring country of Blefescu is drawn into the conflict. Gulliver, who is, of course, a giant in comparison to the tiny Lilliputians, is pressed into service as a secret weapon and averts a potentially disastrous invasion. He wades into the sea and steals away the Blefescan navy before they can attack.

As a final reflective exercise, ask the group if they can give any more contemporary, historical or literary examples of 'secret weapons' being employed decisively in a conflict. The group might like to consider:

- the atomic bombs dropped on Nagasaki and Hiroshima towards the end of World War II, effectively ending Japan's role in the hostilities;
- the machine gun used by the British against the Zulu Nation to terrifying effect during the Boer War;
- the longbow used by the English against the French at the battle of Agincourt;
- the Trojan Horse used to smuggle an army into the gates of Troy.

As a last thought, ask the students to consider whether such a final ending to a major conflict or war necessarily brings peace. It might be true that hostilities and fighting stop, but is this 'peace' or merely a ceasefire until the next conflict starts?

Write the word 'peace' on the board and hand out to each student a piece of paper. Ask them to write one word or phrase that they think best describes what an effective, lasting peace actually is. The students might like to list what people have to actually do to achieve this. What qualities, skills or traits will the people have to bring to the negotiating table?

If you still have the original graffiti wall from Activity 4, asking the students to stick their responses on their – or the other group's – wall offers an interesting and visual contrast highlighting the gulf that might exist between conflict and resolution.

LILLIPUT

Resource sheet I

Eyewitness accounts of a strange land

[1]

These people are most excellent mathematicians, and can work out incredible sums. The Emperor encourages his people and is a great supporter of all types of learning.

[2]

There are people who are called rope dancers who perform their dance on a tightrope of a slender white thread. They perform in front of the Emperor and begin to learn their art when they are very young. If an important job becomes available in the Emperor's court, they will try to get the job by performing a dance . . . Whoever dances the best and jumps the highest without falling, is given the job.

[3]

When the people of this land die, they are buried upside down with their head pointing down and their feet pointing up. They believe that in eleven thousand moons all the dead people will become alive again and the world – which they think is flat – will turn upside down. In this way, they will all be found standing on their feet. Some of the clever people admit this is a silly thing to do, but they continue to do it just the same.

[4]

If a person commits a crime, then they will be punished very harshly. But if the accused person is found not guilty, it is the accuser who is put to death and anything he owns is given to the innocent person to make amends for the inconvenience and hardship of any time spent in jail.

[5]

In the courts of law, the image of justice is a statue with six eyes. Two at the front, two at the side and two behind. This shows that the courts of law must be cautious. The statue carries a bag of gold in her right hand, and a sword in its cover in her left hand to show she is happier rewarding people than punishing them.

[6]

Their children are treated very differently from the way we treat our children. Fathers and mothers have little say in their children's school or education. In fact, children are taught that they do not have to be grateful to their parents for anything. All the children are sent to nurseries and schools in the town. Children are sent to schools that are matched to their families' importance in society, in this way rich and important children are all taught together.

[7]

Young women are just like young men and do not like to be called cowards or fools. They also do not like wearing fancy clothes or jewellery.

[8]

The poorer people who work, live in the cottages and keep their children at home rather than sending them to schools. They teach them how to be farmers. Old people and people who are sick or poorly are looked after by hospitals. This means there are no beggars on the streets in this land.

LILLIPUT

Resource sheet 2

Conflict and war

It began upon the following occasion. It is allowed on all hands, that the primitive way of breaking eggs before we eat them, was upon the larger end: but his present Majesty's grandfather, while he was a boy, going to eat an egg, and breaking it according to the ancient practice, happened to cut one of his fingers. Whereupon the Emperor his father published an edict, commanding all his subjects, upon great penalties, to break the smaller end of their eggs. The people so highly resented this law, that our histories tell us there have been six rebellions raised on that account; wherein one Emperor lost his life, and another his crown . . . it is computed, that eleven thousand persons have, at several times, suffered death, rather than submit to break their eggs at the smaller end.

Unit 6

The White Rose

Introduction and context

> Somebody, after all, had to make a start. What we wrote and said is also believed by many others. They just don't dare to express themselves as we did.
>
> Sophie Scholl at her trial

1943. In a Munich court, brother and sister Hans and Sophie Scholl, with their best friend Christoph Probst, are tried for speaking out against the Nazi regime.

As German teenagers in the 1930s the Scholl siblings had supported Hitler and his rise to power. They had even been members of German youth organisations and, like many others, believed that Hitler was leading Germany into a glorious future.

However, as World War II began and the reality of Hitler's policies became apparent, Sophie and Hans Scholl started to act. Copies of a leaflet called *The White Rose* appeared at the University of Munich. This anonymous essay condemned the Nazi regime and encouraged ordinary Germans to rise up and resist the authority of their own leaders. Such open rebellion was unheard of. Over the next few months, five more leaflets followed. Seeing The White Rose movement begin to attract public support, the Gestapo redoubled their efforts to hunt down the ringleaders.

18 February 1943 saw Hans and Sophie arrested after leaving leaflets in the buildings of the Munich University. Christoph Probst was linked to the movement and also arrested. After four days of interrogation by the Gestapo, they were tried for treason, found guilty and executed on 22 February 1943. Hans was 24 years old, Sophie 21 and Christoph was 22.

More arrests, trials and executions followed as other members of this small group were rounded up. However, even though The White Rose had been broken, its ideals of freedom and non-violent resistance continued to influence many German citizens. Today, the story of The White Rose is taught and celebrated in schools and colleges all over modern Germany.

In this unit, students will have the opportunity to explore the story of The White Rose from a variety of perspectives. They will investigate something of the background context of national socialist Germany in the 1930s and 1940s before dramatising aspects of the White Rose story itself. They will work in both realistic and more abstract modes of performance and will also be able to examine the work of a professional playwright dealing with the same themes. Key issues of representation in drama will be considered as students create their own dramatisations based on carefully structured approaches to this engaging but in some ways problematic material. Finally they will be able to reflect on what they have experienced as they undertake the task of memorialising a group of university students who 'made a start' in resisting oppression.

We anticipate that a group exploring all the activities in this unit would take about eight one-hour lessons to complete the tasks.

The White Rose **unit map**

Activity	Description	Resources	Teacher notes
Activity 1	'Resistance' brainstorm.		
Activity 2	Introduction of photo of Jewish people: questioning. Tableaux and thought tracking of spectators. Captions. Teacher in role to animate images.	Resource sheets 1, 2	
Activity 3	Minimalism and montage: (a) select section to dramatise; (b) construct animated tableaux; (c) choreograph performance.	Resource sheet 3	
Activity 4	Memorials.		
Activity 5	Opening scenes to a commemorative play.		
Activity 6	First meeting: tension – naturalism.	Resource sheets 4a, 4b, 8	
Activity 7	Spreading the word – stylised episodes in four groups: cross-cutting.	Resource sheet 5	
Activity 8	Heroes and villains: hotseating Mohr.		
Activity 9	Game structure – hunt for The White Rose.		
Activity 10	Capture – stylised scenes.	Resource sheet 6	
Activity 11	Script extract – interrogation of Sophie Scholl.	Resource sheet 7	
Activity 12	Final scene of a White Rose 'film'.		
Activity 13	Montage poem – reflection.		

Activity 1

Write the word 'resistance' on the board.

- *What does the word 'resistance' mean to you?*
- *Can anyone think of an example of a person or a group who have stood up for something that they have believed in? This could be a local, national or global occurrence.*
- *How do people make their feelings known when they want to protest against something or stop something from happening?*
- *Can you think of any examples of people putting themselves at risk through their actions as they protest against something?*
- *If 'non-violent' is added to the word 'resistance', what does this phrase imply about the sort of action people might take?*
- *What sort of things would you be willing to fight for – freedom, equality, justice?*

Activity 2

Using Resource sheet 1 (page 126), show the students the photograph of Jewish civilians being forced to clean the streets in Vienna. Without explaining the context of the photograph, encourage them to deconstruct what is happening.

- *When do you think this photograph was taken?*
- *What does it show?*
- *Who are the people on their hands and knees?*
- *Who are the people standing round watching?*

Your students may well successfully place the image in its proper context. However, they might need some more historical information to understand its implications (see box).

Once Hitler and his National Socialist party were established in Germany of the 1930s he began a policy of intolerance and persecution resulting eventually in a process of mass extermination that would become known as 'The Final Solution'.

Hitler was obsessed with creating a master race of Aryans who were blond, blue-eyed, strong and healthy. He said that Germans and other north European people belonged to this Aryan race and should fulfil their destiny of ruling the world. Fuelled by relentless propaganda, the hatred and persecution of any non-Aryan grew. Jews, Slavs (from eastern Europe), black people, communists, gypsies, people with disabilities, homosexuals and anyone who did not hold the views of National Socialism became an enemy of the state.

In the run up to World War II, Jewish people in Germany found themselves in an increasingly dangerous world. Their shops and businesses were destroyed and they were openly attacked. Their houses and goods were seized and confiscated by the state. Laws were passed that banned them from working in government, using public transport or parks or even owning a bicycle. Jews and non-Jews were not allowed to marry each other.

1939 saw Germany plunged into World War II – a war that Hitler waged on two fronts. While German soldiers fought on the battlefields of Europe against the Allies, the persecution of Hitler's enemies at home and in captured countries moved towards its final phase. Whole areas of cities became walled-up Jewish ghettos where thousands starved to death or died of disease. The construction of death camps such as Auschwitz, Sobibor and Treblinka provided the means to the Nazis' 'Final Solution' – intended to be the ultimate destruction of the Jewish people. Six million Jewish people were shipped in cattle trucks to these camps and gassed to death in enormous sealed chambers. An estimated five million further people, from other groups that Hitler persecuted, were also killed in this way.

Arrange some chairs or blocks in the middle of the room and explain that these represent the Jewish people in the photograph being forced to scrub the streets. Ask the students to get into groups of five or six and place each group in a circle around the blocks or chairs. Give each group a piece of paper and a pen.

> *Imagine that you are one of the people in the crowd who find themselves witnessing this event. In your groups, I want you to form a still image of these spectators.*
>
> * *What are your feelings about what is happening?*
> * *Do you think it is fair?*
> * *Are you worried that next time it could be you that is treated this way?*
> * *Do the children in the crowd understand what is happening?*
> * *Can you show your thoughts and feelings through your facial expression and body language?*

Once the students have completed their task, ask them to add a word or phrase that attempts to capture the feelings of their character.

> *I want you to write these words or phrases on the paper I have given you. We will be using them later in the work.*

Allow a few minutes to complete the task, asking each group to incorporate their spoken lines into their still image. As each group presents their drama, encourage the audience to offer captions or titles for each piece of work. Once all groups have shared their work, explain that during the next activity, you are going to work in role alongside them.

> *For this part of the work, I am going to take on a role and become part of your scene. Each group will recreate their still image for a few seconds until I approach in role. As I speak to you, animate your image. Carry the action on with movement and language, reacting to me and to each other until I stop the work. Imagine the play button on a video recorder has just been pressed to make the paused image come alive.*

The choice of role is up to you as the teacher. You may wish to consider a neutral role with equal status to the others in the group, drawing responses and reactions without providing a model to follow. You may wish to introduce the idea that there would be people in the crowd who believe they could be the next victim. A high status 'authority' role might be able to challenge the views of any spectators who might consider voicing their protests at what is going on. By careful questioning, you will be able to build the tension in the scene, highlighting the very serious implications of this event.

* *What's going on here?*
* *Who are the people on their hands and knees?*
* *Why are you letting this happen?*
* *Shouldn't someone do something?*
* *How would you feel if it was you and your family?*
* *It's not fair that these people are treated like this.*
* *I've heard the soldiers saying they are looking for others in the crowd.*
* *This is not the first time this has happened.*
* *If they are doing this now, what will they do next?*
* *Move back, we need to make more room so everyone can see.*
* *It is about time we made examples of these people.*
* *You look sorry for them, would you like to join your friends?*

Allow each group the opportunity to complete this task and discuss the work.

- *What did it feel like to be the spectator of this degrading act?*
- *What do you imagine it might have felt like to be one of the victims?*
- *Identify a line or word that someone said in role that you thought was effective. Why was it effective?*
- *Choose someone whose body language, facial expression, use of voice communicated something important to the audience. What can we learn from this?*

Explain to your students that this drama exploration will be placed within the context of Hitler's Germany, a time of great upheaval for the whole of Europe. Distribute Resource sheet 2 (page 127) and discuss the issues involved.

- *Why were the German authorities determined to stop The White Rose?*
- *What do you think The White Rose represented to ordinary Germans?*
- *What words would you use to describe the leaders of The White Rose?*

Activity 3

If you have followed the introductory work to this point, you now have an option. You can skip this section and rejoin the sequence of work indicated in Activity 4, or include the following tasks. There are two reasons for including these optional activities. First, it serves as extension work for students who have completed the previous activities and now wish to create a more formal performance piece, based on their emerging understanding of The White Rose. Second, for older or more experienced students, this highly structured performance approach may extend their understanding of drama form and encourage them to view the theme from different perspectives.

This extension work raises interesting questions about the relationship between drama form and content. By moving the students into performance at this relatively early stage in the project, interesting questions about the relationship between process drama and theatre are explored.

In this sequence of activities students will explore the concept of minimalism in the arts in order to create a montage-style performance based around fragments of The White Rose story as introduced in the previous frames. The form of the performance is stylised and without words, which has proved to be a highly effective way for students to consider the treatment of heightened emotion in theatre, paradoxically, by reducing the theatre form to its barest essentials.

Explain to the group that they are going to dramatise the story of The White Rose (as detailed in Resource sheet 2, page 127) in a very specific way. The work will proceed by drawing on ideas found most obviously in the visual arts and music – within the twentieth-century art movement known as minimalism.

> Minimalism focuses on presenting an idea that has been distilled to its essence and could be summed up by the credo 'less means more'. Musicians who have used these principles in their work are Steve Reich, Phillip Glass, Michael Nyman and Arvo Part. In the visual arts, presenting the paintings of Bridget Riley or the sculptures of Carl Andre may help students understand some of the principles involved. As a literary parallel, the Haiku verse form is a very accessible illustration.

Assemble the pupils into groups of four or five and ask them to select one episode from The White Rose story (using Resource sheet 3, page 128), and help them to choose a moment that they see as significant, perhaps based around a key image, or a specific moment of heightened tension. In order to dramatise this episode, the groups are going to find a dramatic equivalent to the Haiku verse or Carl Andre's bricks, by creating a movement motif using the technique of 'animated tableau'.

Ask the group to imagine a videotape that has been paused. A frozen picture exists on the television screen. By pressing the frame advance button, the picture changes almost imperceptibly. By then reversing the process – so the image returns back to its original position – a very short moment in time is captured, advanced and then reversed. In their groups, the pupils will explore this technique starting with a still image and manipulating their image forwards and backwards 'frame by frame' through extremely small, subtle movements. By repeating this 'single frame' animation perhaps three or four times, and by carefully choreographing the movement, it is possible to achieve highly resonant and absorbing effects, which explore human relationships, feelings and motivation in a very subtle manner.

The pupils should be encouraged to experiment with the pace of their 'repeats', and reduce the size of their movements to that necessary to capture the essence of the moment they are dramatising. Eye contact, facial expression and gesture should be refined, so that everything that is presented on stage is deliberate, and carefully contrived. A challenging aspect of this work is in choreographing the various components of the animated tableaux to extract as much meaning from the scene as possible. For instance, in a motif based around an episode when Hans Scholl provocatively shook hands with a group of Jews who had been loaded onto cattle trucks by the Nazis, one group of students carefully synchronised their movement to good effect: as Hans offered his hand towards the prisoners in the truck, each of them responded differently. One, looking Hans directly in the eye, moved to grasp his hand as though grateful; a second, aware of the German soldier observing them, looked away and ignored the proffered handshake. A third, as if unable to decide what to do, simply looked from one prisoner to the other. All of this was signalled with subtle, repeated gestures, carefully timed to maximum effect.

As soon as the groups have created their tableaux and repeated movements, they should choose another two episodes to dramatise in the same way. Once each group has created three animated tableaux, representing three different fragments of The White Rose story, their work can be presented as a dramatic montage or sequence. Ask the groups to consider the order in which they wish to present their tableaux. Designate an acting area and seat the groups on chairs around its edge, either 'in the round' or 'traverse' (on two sides). Invite the groups to rehearse their entrance into the stage area for each of their movement motifs. In this form of theatre, very small actions or events can become quite significant, including the way actors enter or leave the performance area.

Once a group has performed its first animated tableau they return to their chairs, which becomes the cue for the next group to perform. When each group has performed their first movement motif, the sequence continues through motifs two and three, until all the work is performed. Design elements such as lighting and sound can add a great deal to the dramatic effect of this work. Music especially can enhance the emotive impact on the audience. By experimenting with the use of music as a soundtrack – such as Arvo Part's *Speigel Im Speigel* from *Alina* – students can create effective and moving performances.

Activity 4

Regardless of the pathway you have followed to reach this point in the project, the students should now have a growing understanding of the achievements and actions of The White Rose. Once the students are in groups of four or five, introduce the following:

> *If a group of people wanted to commemorate and remember what The White Rose achieved, what would serve as a fitting memorial? What might have people thought of The White Rose at the time? Do you think that it might be different to the way that people think of them now?*

Discuss the suggestions from the group. They might include making a statue or sculpture, creating a painting, mural or poster, composing and performing a song, writing a poem or even creating a play or piece of drama.

Ask each group to create a memorial that is to be placed on the spot where the Scholls were arrested. You might wish to steer the students towards creating an image that is abstract – representing the idea of resistance symbolically. Examples could be a clenched fist, a group menacingly towering over a lone crouching figure, a crowd making the same gesture while one person does something differently.

Allow each group time to create their memorial and share them in turn. Ask each group to presents their work. Evaluate the task by encouraging the students to consider:

- *Which was the most powerful presentation?*
- *Why was it powerful?*
- *Was there an image that captured the ideas behind The White Rose?*

Activity 5

Ask the group to consider the following. If they were devising a play to commemorate The White Rose, and the memorials shaped in Activity 4 were to be the basis of the opening scene, how could they use them in the drama to create a powerful start to the play? As the pupils move into performance mode, they will need to consider what they are trying to communicate to the audience in this opening scene.

- Does the group have an audience in mind when starting to create their drama?
- How will this affect the way they will develop their performance?
- What effect should the opening scene have on the audience? Should it create a mood or atmosphere, introduce the theme or plot, introduce characters or set the time and place of the action?
- Is the opening scene important to introduce the style and form of the drama to the audience?
- Where will the audience be in relation to the action on the stage?

The following are suggestions that would encourage the students to shape their previous work into a more multi-dimensional scene. You may wish to empower one of the students to take on the role of director. The role of the director is to help co-ordinate the whole class in reinterpreting the selected piece of work.

Ask the group to select an effective example from the previous task.

- *If we were going to re-shape this work, making sure that everyone in the class is included, how could we make sure that we do not lose the elements that make it work so well?*
- *If this is the beginning of the play, how as actors might you build this group image on stage?*

Encourage the class to experiment:

- Each actor walks onto stage individually, building the image person by person.
- As a group, all the actors converge onto the stage and create the image.

Ask the group what they can do to support this movement and make it dramatically more effective.

- Incorporate the words or phrases that each group wrote down in Activity 2.
- Use a narrator to read out a speech written from the perspective of one of the characters.
- Experiment using different ways of moving onto the stage. For instance, what might be the different effects created by entering quickly, whilst looking directly at the audience or, alternatively, moving in a slow, deliberate manner with heads bowed?
- Experiment with vocal effects such as chanting, whispering or singing. Text can be selected from any of the work covered so far and might include extracts from the leaflets of The White Rose, facts or dates that the students have learnt or words actually spoken in drama created by the students themselves.

- Play recorded music that evokes the time or theme and creates an atmosphere.
- Use live percussion or instruments.
- Introduce lighting to emphasise and highlight different areas of the stage.

The scene could involve one group creating the first image; another forming the second and so on until three or four images are presented. Again, all the different ways of supporting the scene could be discussed and tried out.

Activity 6

Gather the students into a circle. Ask them to imagine the very first meeting of The White Rose. What dangers might they have faced? It is important to emphasise the extreme risks that these young people were taking just by discussing any sort of protest. Using Resource sheets 4a and 4b (pages 129 and 130), ask the students to consider the following:

- *Where do you think they might have met?*
- *As it was so dangerous to openly criticise Hitler and the Nazi Party, how do you think the idea of a resistance movement was first proposed?*
- *What do you think the group actually wanted to achieve?*
- *How did they arrive at the idea of printing and distributing leaflets?*
- *As it would take only one person to inform on the others, did they take an oath of secrecy to protect each other's names?*
- *What worries might the group have had?*
- *Was everyone willing to take such a personal risk and defy the authorities?*

Write the words 'dramatic tension' on the board. Again, reinforce the idea that the young people of The White Rose were taking enormous personal risks in embarking upon their course of passive resistance. If caught, they would face imprisonment and even death. Any improvisation showing this imagined first meeting must create a sense of tension for the audience. You may need to help define dramatic tension for the students. A 'checklist' (Resource sheet 8, page 134), is provided that may be helpful in explaining how tension in drama is created. In addition there are a number of children's games with which the class may be familiar which are based on the principle of dramatic tension:

- *Grandmother's Footsteps*;
- *Wink Murder*;
- *Blind Man's Buff*;
- *Keeper of the Keys*.

Once the content and context of the improvisation have been explored, ask the students to consider the dramatic elements of the scene, explaining that they are to use naturalistic drama as a style.

> *Naturalistic theatre came about as some playwrights and directors wanted to accurately reproduce the social world on stage – with all the problems and complexities that that entails. It is often described as showing a 'slice of life' on stage. The acting style means that actors try to show their emotions and feelings in as real and believable a manner as possible. Thinking about this particular scene:*
>
> - *How are you going to portray your characters?*
> - *How much of this characterisation is to be based on fact, and how much is imagination?*
> - *How can your group introduce tension into the scene?*
> - *How will the scene start and finish? How will this influence the tension created in the scene?*

Ask the students to form mixed gender groups of five. Explain that they will have 15 minutes to develop the scene, which should last around three minutes.

Once the pupils have shared the work, evaluate and discuss.

- *What are the difficulties faced by actors and directors who have to portray people who actually lived?*
- *Do we have a responsibility to be as accurate as possible when we are representing them on stage?*

Activity 7

Explain to the students that in this workshop they will be looking at ways of representing the spreading of the ideas in The White Rose leaflets and building an understanding of the risks the group members were taking at the time. Present to the class some of the quotations from the actual leaflets (Resource sheet 5, page 131). Explain that in the early years of World War II, much of Germany was in a state of confusion. Many people were fearful for their lives and their livelihood, and many ordinary Germans had had to make difficult decisions as to where their allegiances lay.

If there are sufficient numbers in the class, the students could divide into four groups, each devising different prepared improvisations and then finding a way of linking the drama into a complete scene involving everyone. Alternatively, the whole group could tackle each improvisation in turn.

Some of these scenes will use stylised drama, which attempts to represent characters or events in a symbolic or abstract manner. Mime and movement are often features of stylised drama, as is using language in a creative way – perhaps through choral speaking or creating a soundscape. In this form of theatre, the relationship between the actor and the audience is often different from that found in realistic drama.

Group 1

The members of The White Rose used a hand operated duplicating machine to print their leaflets. This was a dangerous business and had to be done in complete secrecy. Often working at night and in secret locations, they would print thousands of leaflets to distribute. Some of the leaflets were left in places where lots of people gathered. Some of them were posted to people picked out of the telephone directory. They often targeted village and town pubs, as well as universities as places where they thought their ideas might be discussed.

Explain that the students are to create a stylised improvisation of the different parts of the hand operated duplicating machine using mime and movement. These could be the turning of the hand crank, inking the typeset, loading paper, folding, addressing and posting the leaflets to different areas in Germany.

- Using Resource sheet 5, how could they include quotations from the actual leaflets into their stylised scene?
- How could they ensure that there is a sense of tension in the scene? For instance, how might they imply the fear of informers, of being discovered, being followed to the secret location, or of having to work quickly and quietly?

Group 2

The members of The White Rose would copy, at random, names from telephone directories and use the postal system to spread their ideas all over Germany. Remembering that it was both illegal and very dangerous to criticise Hitler and his policies, imagine what it might have felt like to receive one of the leaflets. Would people be frightened of being associated with The White Rose – in case they were called traitors? Would some people be angry, seeing it as being unpatriotic and against Germany? Or do you think some people might agree with the leaflets and be glad that people were finally speaking out?

Ask the group to create a prepared improvisation that shows a number of different reactions to people picking up or receiving the leaflets in the post.

- Using Resource sheet 5, how could they incorporate quotations from the actual leaflets into their scene?
- If the group organises itself by breaking down into pairs or threes to show the different reactions, how could they link these elements of the scene? By using still images? By using the same statement from the leaflets repeated in each reaction? By using a single piece of paper passed from pair to pair to symbolise the leaflet?

Group 3

A few months before they were finally arrested, Hans Scholl, Alexander Schmorell and Willi Graff staged a daring protest. Over three nights they used bitumen paint and brushes to daub slogans on the sides of houses on one of the main roads near Munich University. They wrote 'Down With Hitler', 'Hitler Mass Murderer', 'Freedom', and drew crossed-out swastikas. They did this despite the fact that the police had redoubled their efforts to catch the protesters and were patrolling the streets. If they were caught it would mean certain arrest and very possibly execution, but their gesture very publicly presented their ideas.

Ask the students to consider how they could represent these events. Considering the dangers involved, there is great scope in this scene to explore the creation of dramatic tension. For instance, splitting the action on stage between the authorities and the three men of The White Rose might give opportunities to build tension by showing events happening at the same time: one group might show an officer briefing a patrol, while the other shows the protestors quickly daubing paint.

Group 4

Once the dangerous activity of printing the leaflets had been accomplished, an even more hazardous activity – that of distribution – had to be undertaken. The group would often pack leaflets into suitcases and travel by train to outlying towns and villages. In the event of the train being searched by the police, they would place the suitcases on the luggage rack and hide in the toilet or move to another compartment. These journeys could become very risky and sometimes extremely tense affairs.

How could the students show the imagined inner thoughts of the people involved in their drama? The action could freeze at points, allowing a few characters to 'step out' of the action and briefly speak their thoughts directly to the audience before moving back into the action. This technique is often referred to as 'stepping out.'

Once the students are happy with each improvisation and they have been refined and developed through rehearsal and evaluation, they can be considered to be viable scenes in the play.

The group working as directors needs to consider the following:

- Are all the scenes to be included? Are some scenes more relevant than others? Are some more dramatically effective than others? Does each scene communicate something to the audience, or are some parts confusing or not clear? Sometimes improvisations created in the exploration phases will not make it through to the performance phase.

- What would be a successful order for the scenes to follow? Although the scenes should create an overall picture when put together, they do not develop one chronological narrative that grows event by event. The improvisations stand alone and are like a *montage* – a collection of thematically linked scenes that support each other to create a dramatic whole. To create links between the individual scenes, the technique of cross-cutting can be used to move to different moments in different scenes.

  Now we have created a series of scenes, we can make links between them by using a technique called cross-cutting. This is when we re-order the events in the scenes by 'cutting' forwards and backwards to different moments. If there is a moment that we really want to emphasise to the audience, we can repeat it at different times. We could also place two contrasting events side by side to highlight the differences to the audience. This is called juxtaposition.

It is probably useful to use a large piece of sugar paper to plan out the cross-cutting sequences. Identify the running order of the scenes using a key word or title and write in the cue lines for the next section. This visual aid might help make the concept clear to the students and make rehearsing the complete scene easier.

Activity 8

Introduce the idea that in order for the pupils to understand what The White Rose movement was attempting to achieve, the group ought to look at the people who were responsible for trying to stop them.

This opens up a whole area of discussion on how the students might portray the perceived 'heroes' and 'villains' in this true story.

- Ask the pupils to make a list of fictional villains they have come across in films, television and books. How are they portrayed? Are there examples of common traits that these villains share – physical appearance, behaviour, gestures, voice, accent, gender? Can the group develop a stereotyped image of a villain? Is this image accurate? Can anyone think of a villain who is portrayed as being a 'normal' person?

  To continue this exploration further, we are going to use hotseating. By directly questioning someone in role, we will be able to build up a picture of the character or the event we are exploring. We might use this information to create a scene or to help us understand and portray characters in more detail.

Explain that you are going to take on the role of a high-ranking Gestapo officer called Mohr, who was trying to track down the members of The White Rose. Reminding them of their previous discussion about stereotypes, ask the group to direct you in acting out the role. Once the group has established how the character should be portrayed, allow some time for them to formulate some questions they will ask.

Place a chair in the circle and conduct the hotseating session. It may be useful to evaluate the exercise at the end:

- *Did it help us to understand more about why the authorities wanted The White Rose stopped?*
- *Were the questions answered truthfully?*
- *Do you think that is what the real Mohr might have been like?*

Activity 9

Perhaps it was always inevitable that the young members of The White Rose would get caught. For this part of the workshop we are going to create a scene that shows the authorities and their attempts to find The White Rose members. There are a number of different ways that we can show this.

> *As a whole group we are now going to use stylised or symbolic theatre to represent the authorities and their quest to capture the Scholls and the other members of the group.*

Ask the group to consider children's games as a starting point for this improvisation. Can they list games that include chases or involve hiding or finding people? In the game *What's the Time, Mr Wolf?* one player stands facing a wall with her back to the 'wolves'. Their objective is to creep forward and grab their victim, but every time she turns round, the wolves have to freeze. Anyone moving is sent to the back to start again.

> *Is there a way that we could adapt a children's game to show the authorities closing in on The White Rose? The real danger for the young people of The White Rose would contrast well with the innocence of a children's game.*
>
> *How are we going to portray the Gestapo and members of the Nazi party – as faceless, anonymous figures or as 'real' people? Perhaps we could use the space in an imaginative manner to show their power and status? Perhaps they have a gesture, movement or chant that is repeated as they move in to surround The White Rose?*

Once the pupils have created their improvisations, share the work.

> *How could we improve the way in which the audience is drawn in through the action of the scene? Tension is linked with pace, so could we introduce a way of varying the pace of the scene from start to finish? Perhaps this could be achieved by using percussion, sound, words or movement that builds steadily during the scene?*

Activity 10

Read out the following account that details the capture of Hans and Sophie Scholl as they secretly left leaflets in the University of Munich.

> *On Thursday 18 February 1943, Hans and Sophie Scholl made their way to the University of Munich buildings carrying a suitcase of White Rose leaflets. As they made their way through the building, they dropped leaflets in the deserted corridors. Knowing that any minute students would come flooding out of their lectures, they made their way out of the building. Outside they found a stack of leaflets at the bottom of their suitcase. Taking an enormous risk, they headed back into the University and climbed a staircase that overlooked the inner courtyard. Hurling the leaflets into the air, they fell to the ground below just as the students arrived. Unfortunately, the University handyman Jakob Schmidt, who was a Nazi Party member, had spotted them. He alerted the authorities and the couple were easily arrested and taken away by the Gestapo for questioning.*

Ask the group to consider ways to represent this sequence of events in a stylised, physical way. How could they show the Scholls hurriedly walking down corridors, depositing their leaflets?

Possible ideas that students might develop further are:

- The majority of the group forms a corridor, while two students in role as Hans and Sophie walk between them 'dropping leaflets'.
- Use stage blocks at various levels to represent Hans and Sophie on the staircase.
- Use sheets of paper to represent the leaflets showering down upon the students below.
- The rest of the group forms a still image of the students coming out of their lectures. As the leaflets settle, the still image could change from being a group of students, to the police who make the arrest.

Using still image as a controlling device in this sequence should avoid a 'chase and arrest' scene but will need careful structuring so that the narrative thread is clear to the audience.

For the final section it may be appropriate to introduce a narrator. Ask a student to take on the role of Jakob Schmidt, the university handyman who alerted the authorities. He or she could describe the events from their point of view as the 'hero of the hour'. An example of a possible speech is suggested in Resource sheet 6 (page 132).

Activity 11

We are going to look at a scene from a play that is based on the events of The White Rose. In this scene, the captive Sophie Scholl is interrogated for the first time by Mohr, a high-ranking Gestapo officer.

Organise the group into a circle and invite three students who will read the parts of Sophie Scholl, Mohr and Bauer. Instruct the students playing Mohr and Bauer (the guard) to perform in the circle. Place a chair for the student playing Sophie Scholl.

As you watch the scene, see if you can decide which character has the highest status: who has most power over the situation or the other characters in the scene?

Allow the actors to perform the extract (Resource sheet 7, page 133) from start to finish. Hand out copies of the script to the rest of the group and discuss the scene.

- What does the group think the author is trying to achieve in this scene? What is she trying communicate to the audience? What is the style of the scene – is it 'naturalistic' or 'stylised' theatre?
- Who has the highest status in the scene? The situation suggests that it should be Mohr as he is in charge and asking all the questions. Are there moments when the status changes, perhaps when Sophie Scholl manages to evade the questions, explains the empty suitcase or quotes (in uncomfortable detail) from the leaflets' description of Hitler?
- What does the group think of Mohr's attitude towards his young female captive? What clues are there to show his prejudices about young women and the kind of activities that are suitable for them?
- How does Sophie use Mohr's preconceptions about women to gain the upper hand?
- At the end of the scene, who seems to have the most status?
- In the scene Mohr has not been able to get Sophie to admit to the crime: she has explained her actions, called Hitler a mass murderer, and remained pleasant and seemingly naive about the graveness of her situation. What effect does this seem to have on Mohr?

Ask the students to consider how they would portray the characters on stage. For instance, should Sophie be portrayed as:

- Apologetic?
- Frightened?
- Anxious?
- Agitated?

- Calm?
- At ease?
- Pretending to be as helpful as she can?

Does her demeanour change at points in the scene? Can the students identify these key 'transitions'?

Alternatively, should Mohr be played as:

- Angry?
- Forceful?
- Aggressive?

- Flustered?
- Relaxed and composed?
- Conciliatory?

What effect might these different interpretations have upon the scene?

Does his attitude towards Sophie change during the scene? Can the students pinpoint these changes, and suggest why they have occurred?

Are there moments in the scene when the pace of the action changes? What is implied by the pauses in the dialogue? How do all these factors affect the atmosphere and mood of the scene?

> *There are many different ways that this scene could be interpreted and performed. In theatre, this is often achieved through the actor and the director working together. One of the jobs of the director is to help the actor make decisions about how best to present their character on stage. Working in groups of four, assign one person to be the director and create your own version of this scene.*

Allow the groups some time to prepare their work. You may wish to divide the scene into sections and assign each group a section to perform.

Activity 12

Explain that the group is now going to conclude the exploration of The White Rose.

> *Along with Hans and Sophie Scholl, Christoph Probst was arrested. After four days of intensive interrogation they faced their accusers in court. The trial lasted only a few hours and as the three defendants had admitted their involvement, no witnesses were called. Proceedings ended with Roland Freisler, Chief Justice of the Peoples Court of the Greater German Reich, pronouncing all three guilty of treason. Their sentence was the death penalty.*
>
> *The accused were taken back to prison where Hans and Sophie were allowed a final visit from their parents. All three prisoners then met briefly before they were individually led to the guillotine.*
>
> *To cement their victory and make sure that all resistance was crushed, the Gestapo continued to investigate The White Rose. As they gathered information, more arrests were made and executions were carried out.*

Ask the group to imagine that they are a cinema production team who have been making a film about The White Rose. They must now consider what to include as the final scene of the film.

- Why is the final scene of any play or film important?
- How important is it to communicate a mood or atmosphere to an audience?
- Do they want to leave the audience with a sense of despair, or hope and well-being?
- How might they achieve an 'uplifting' ending, when the end of The White Rose was so tragic?

Can the students make links with other groups or individuals who have protested passively or made sacrifices against injustice or intolerance? These could be contemporary examples that remind us that struggle and protest against oppression are not just confined to history.

- Is there scope to return to an earlier image or scene and use this as the closing sequence of the piece?
- Considering the style of the scene, would the group favour a broadly stylised or more realistic approach?

Once the students have discussed these issues and considered different approaches, allow them time to shape the scene, either working as a whole group or in smaller groups. An effective way of concluding this work while allowing the students to work in a different medium is to use a video camera to record the finished scene. If the students are presenting their work in a final performance, this short video extract could be incorporated into the live performance – perhaps as an 'epilogue'.

Activity 13

This final activity – the creation of a communal poem based on a montage of 'texts' already explored in the drama – may enable pupils to reflect upon the meaning of their work, and give a degree of 'closure' to the unit of work.

Ask each student to select a word or phrase – significant to them – from all of the work so far explored in The White Rose unit, and to write their phrase on a separate sheet of paper using capital letters and a broad felt tip.

The sheets are now arranged in a single line on the floor. In this way a kind of random 'poem' has been created.

Explain to the group that the class will now re-arrange the order of the phrases that make up the poem, in order to create something more structured and intentional. Each pupil is, however, only allowed to make two 'moves'. If necessary the 'poem' can be split into two or three sections in order to make adjustments easier to manage. Once the pupils have made their adjustments to the poem, the sheets are numbered in order to record the final order.

Each pupil reclaims their original sheet that is now numbered, and standing in a circle, the class collaboratively read their poem. This reading can be then polished in various ways:

- Pupils can learn their phrases, and by memorising which pupil reads before them, the sheets can be discarded.
- The group can experiment with dynamics, tone, pitch, rhythm, etc. in order to create mood and atmosphere.
- By 'framing' the reading of the poem (as part of a *memorial service* or as an *elegy*, for instance) aspects of ritual can be explored.

As a final moment which might provide a suitably atmospheric end to the unit, experiment with a ritualised performance of the poem whilst re-enacting the memorials to The White Rose created in Activity 4.

THE WHITE ROSE

Resource sheet 1

THE WHITE ROSE

Resource sheet 2

'Long live freedom.'

These are the words that Hans Scholl uttered just before his execution by the Nazis in February 1943. At the same time, his sister Sophie was also executed along with their friend Christoph Probst.

What made their deaths unusual at a time when thousands of people were dying on the battlefields of World War II was that they were educated young Germans protesting against what their leader Adolf Hitler and his government were doing to their country.

Between the summer of 1942 and February 1943, Hans and Sophie Scholl, with a small group of friends, began to write and distribute a series of pamphlets called *The Leaflets of The White Rose*. These leaflets encouraged ordinary Germans to resist Hitler and to stand up against a government that they thought was sending thousands of Germans needlessly to their deaths.

This was a very dangerous thing to do. It was illegal to openly criticise Hitler or any of his policies. Hitler's police – the Gestapo – were everywhere, and anyone who dared to speak out knew they risked being arrested, tortured and even executed if they were caught.

Meeting secretly, the members of The White Rose would use a hand powered duplicating machine to print out thousands of copies of the leaflets. These would be posted to people all over Germany, or left in places where many people could see them. At the bottom of each leaflet they would ask people to 'make as many copies of this leaflet as you can and distribute them'.

Some members of the movement would even go out late at night and paint graffiti such as 'Down with Hitler' and 'Hitler the Mass Murderer' in large letters on buildings in Munich.

As The White Rose started to gather public support, the Gestapo increased its efforts to find the ringleaders. Eventually they were successful. A member of the Nazi party saw Hans and Sophie Scholl throwing leaflets from the balcony of a large hall in Munich's university.

After being arrested, they were interrogated by the Gestapo for four days and then tried for treason. They were found to be guilty by the court and sentenced to death.

The execution was carried out almost immediately. Other deaths followed as the Gestapo tried to remove all trace of The White Rose and the resistance it represented.

Today, in modern Germany, it is a different story. Germans celebrate the strength and courage of The White Rose movement. A square at the University of Munich is named after Hans and Sophie Scholl and there are schools and streets all over Germany named for each member of the group.

THE WHITE ROSE

Resource sheet 3

[This resource sheet presents fragments of The White Rose story to be used in Activity 3. The incidents are presented in chronological order from the Scholls' family life in the small town of Ulm, to the arrest and subsequent execution of Hans and Sophie.]

1 As a teenager, Hans joins the Hitler Youth. He soon becomes unhappy with their condemnation of all things 'non-German'. At one meeting he has an argument and hits a senior official from the Hitler Youth organisation he belongs to.

2 The Gestapo, alerted by the children's connection with an outlawed youth organisation, arrive at the family home. As the men search the house, Frau Scholl makes the excuse of 'going to the bakers'. She quickly hides incriminating books in her basket and takes them to a neighbour. Nevertheless, Sophie, with her younger sister Inge, and older brother Werner, are arrested and taken away. Hans is arrested later and remains in custody for five weeks.

3 In a symbolic gesture, Werner Scholl leaves the Hitler Youth. To show the blindness of the regime he later ties a swastika scarf around the eyes of a statue standing in front of the town's Law Courts. Werner is eventually to die serving as a soldier at the Russian front.

4 Hans Scholl is conscripted into the German army. Serving as a soldier, he sees Russian and Jewish prisoners being treated badly. In a gesture of solidarity, he gives an old man his tobacco ration. To a young Jewish girl he offers his food. She throws it back. He offers it again, this time with a flower. She accepts and puts the flower in her hair.

5 In another incident Hans shakes hands with Jewish prisoners as they are loaded onto cattle trucks bound for concentration camps.

6 Students at Munich University throw a Nazi speaker out of the lecture hall after he makes lewd comments regarding female members of the student audience. That afternoon there is an anti-Nazi protest on the streets of Munich – reportedly the only public demonstration against the Nazis in the history of the Third Reich.

7 Hans, Sophie and Elisabeth Scholl arrive at Munich University for a lecture by Kurt Huber. Along with the other students, they are confronted with the word 'Freedom' daubed on the wall in thick paint. Some students are angry and speculate as to who is responsible for such an act of defiance. The members of The White Rose, who are present, smile to themselves.

8 On Thursday 18 February 1943, Hans and Sophie hurry through the corridors of the University depositing copies of the sixth and final leaflet. They leave the main building. Finding some spare copies in their suitcase, they re-enter the university, heading for the main staircase. They tip the remaining leaflets into the courtyard below, just as the students stream into the square. Seeing this act, the university's caretaker and Nazi party member, Jakob Schmid, challenges them and seizes each of them by the arm. The Gestapo is called and the Scholls are taken away in handcuffs.

9 Christoph Probst is arrested the next day and stands trial with the Scholls. Despite being a family man with three children, he like the others is sentenced to death.

10 At the trial of Sophie and Hans, their father Robert Scholl has to be escorted from the room after standing up and denouncing the court proceedings.

11 During her four days of interrogation, Sophie Scholl's leg is hurt so badly that she needs crutches to walk to the execution scaffold. Despite the pain, she climbs the steps to the guillotine unaided.

12 As Hans Scholl is escorted to the guillotine, he shouts one last defiant sentence, 'Es lebe die frieheit!' – 'Long live freedom.'

13 Some days later, Professor Huber, a university lecturer and a significant supporter of The White Rose, is arrested and executed along with a number of other students linked to the cause.

14 Copies of The White Rose leaflets eventually find their way to England. They are reprinted and dropped by the thousands by the Royal Air Force during bombing raids over mainland Germany.

THE WHITE ROSE

Resource sheet 4a

The meeting

These are the characters you might wish to include in your scene. Use the descriptions to help you make decisions about how to portray them in your acting.

Hans Scholl: Age 25. As a corporal in the German medical core, he saw the realities of modern warfare and the destructive policies of Hitler. A founder member of The White Rose, he was executed with his sister Sophie on 22 February 1943.

Sophie Scholl: Age 22. Like her brother, Sophie became disillusioned with the fanatical support of Hitler and National Socialism. A keen reader and talented artist, she attended the same university as her brother and there became active with The White Rose.

Alexander Schmorell: Age 26. Called Alex or Shurik by his friends, he was a doctor who had served in the German army at the Russian front. A keen artist, musician and sculptor, he first met Hans Scholl in high school. He was executed on 13 July 1943.

Kurt Huber: Age 40. A philosophy lecturer and Associate Professor at Munich University, he was approached by members of The White Rose for advice. He became involved in the movement and edited the final two leaflets. He was executed with Alexander Schmorell.

Jurgen Wittenstein: Age 26. Jurgen introduced Hans and Alexander and became a very active member of the movement, editing and distributing the leaflets. He escaped the arrests by serving in the front lines of the war. He is still alive and lives in America.

Christoph Probst: Age 24. A medical student and German soldier, Christoph was married with three children. He would write much of the content included in the leaflets. He was tried with Hans and Sophie and executed with them on 22 February 1943 without seeing his newborn third daughter.

Willi Graff: Age 25. Willi was an extremely active member of the group, who wrote a number of the leaflets. Willi also painted slogans and graffiti on buildings at night. He was executed on 12 October 1943 after being interrogated for months by the Gestapo.

THE WHITE ROSE

Resource sheet 4b

The meeting

As a group decide on the following:

- Where are you going to set your scene? Where do you think it would have been safest to meet and discuss such things when they were risking their lives even talking about such matters?
- As it was so dangerous to openly criticise Hitler and the Nazi Party, how do you think they started to discuss the idea of a resistance movement?
- As it would take only one person to inform on the others, did they take an oath of secrecy to protect each other's names?
- What worries might the group have had?
- Was everyone willing to take such a personal risk and defy the authorities?

Try to include the following facts in the scene:

- The aim of The White Rose was to get ordinary citizens to question what Hitler and Germany's leaders were actually doing.
- They thought that by printing and distributing leaflets their message would be spread across the country.
- Being arrested would mean death or being sent to a concentration camp.

Consider the following issues:

- How can you introduce *tension* into the scene?
- How will the scene start and finish?
- What are you trying to *communicate* to the audience in this scene?

THE WHITE ROSE

Resource sheet 5

Extracts from The White Rose *leaflets*

It is certain that today every honest German is ashamed of his government.

Who among us has any conception of the dimensions of shame that will befall us and our children when one day the veil has fallen from our eyes and the most horrible of crimes – crimes that infinitely outdistance every human measure – reach the light of day?

Since the conquest of Poland three hundred thousand Jews have been murdered in this country in the most bestial way.

Jews, too, are human beings.

Why do German people behave so apathetically in the face of all these abominable crimes?

The meaning and the goal of passive resistance is to topple National Socialism, and in this struggle we must not recoil from any course, any action, whatever its nature.

At all points we must oppose National Socialism, wherever it is open to attack. We must soon bring this monster of a state to an end. A victory of fascist Germany in this war would have immeasurable, frightful consequences.

The defeat of the Nazis must unconditionally be the first order of business.

Sabotage in armament plants and war industries, sabotage at all gatherings, rallies, public ceremonies, and organisations of the National Socialist Party.

Neither Hitler nor Goebbels can have counted the dead.

Every word that comes from Hitler's mouth is a lie.

Has God not given you the strength, the will to fight? We must attack evil where it is strongest, and it is strongest in the power of Hitler.

Germans! Do you and your children want to suffer the same fate that befell the Jews?

For us there is but one slogan: fight against the party! We will not be silent. We are your bad conscience. The White Rose will not leave you in peace!

THE WHITE ROSE

Resource sheet 6

Jakob Schmidt's story

I remember it very well. It was Thursday 18 February and of course the year was 1943. I was going about my duties, as I always do, when I saw the man and woman walking down the corridors. The unusual thing that drew my attention was the suitcase they had with them. They also seemed to be nervous – acting in a strange manner – and they were hurrying, as if they were late for a train or something.

A few minutes later, when I saw them at the top of the staircase, I knew something was very wrong. In front of my very eyes I saw them tip up their suitcase and dozens of pieces of paper began falling through the air to the ground below. All this happened just as the students came out of their lectures and poured into the courtyard. Some of the students caught the leaflets as they fell to the ground and began reading them.

I knew what I had to do. After phoning the police, I started locking the doors so that they could not escape. It was over in minutes. They were arrested immediately and taken away. Even then, I had no idea that it was the people who call themselves The White Rose.

THE WHITE ROSE

Resource sheet 7

The White Rose *by Lillian Garrett-Groag*

Act 1 Scene 3

Bauer in brown-shirt uniform, an unthinking face and anodyne grin, escorts Sophie Scholl in. Mohr indicates a chair for her to sit on, and continues to look through the reports while he talks.

MOHR: Name?

SOPHIE: Sophie Scholl.

MOHR: Age?

SOPHIE: Twenty-one.

MOHR: Occupation?

SOPHIE: Student at the University of Munich.

MOHR: What do you study?

SOPHIE: Biology and philosophy.

MOHR: I thought girls went for literature courses.

SOPHIE: Oh, I read a lot of . . .

MOHR: What?

SOPHIE: . . . things. Whatever is allowed – available.

MOHR: Love stories and such?

SOPHIE: *(Pause)* Yes.

MOHR: Do you know what you're accused of?

SOPHIE: Something about some leaflets?

MOHR: You are suspected of co-authoring and distributing a set of pamphlets hostile in the extreme to the Führer, the Reich and the German war effort.

SOPHIE: Goodness.

MOHR: These pamphlets are, naturally, anonymous, and titled 'The White Rose'.

SOPHIE: I know nothing about it, sir. *(Pause)*

MOHR: What were you doing in school? You've no classes today according to your schedule here.

SOPHIE: We decided to go home tonight. To Ulm. We had to let some friends know. *(Beat)* Do you think we'll be able to catch the five o'clock train, sir? If not, I have to call home.

MOHR: You . . . *suddenly* decided to go to Ulm? Why?

SOPHIE: Oh, mother . . . you know how it is.

MOHR: And your entire luggage consists of an empty suitcase.

SOPHIE: What?

MOHR: When you were arrested, you were carrying an empty suitcase.

SOPHIE: Oh, for the laundry.

MOHR: The laundry.

SOPHIE: Mother does our laundry and we pick it up from her. *(Privately)* Hans never washes his own clothes. Disgusting.

MOHR: Yes, well. Sophie . . . is it?

SOPHIE: Yes, sir. *(Very clearly)* Sophia Magdalene Scholl.

MOHR: Sophie, do you know the contents of the pamphlets in question?

SOPHIE: I've seen them around. Everybody has. So I have an idea.

MOHR: And you know what they say.

SOPHIE: . . . I believe they call the Führer a . . . charlatan, and a . . . well, a mass murderer, and a –

MOHR: Ah . . . yes, I –

SOPHIE: . . . and a gangster, and –

MOHR: Yes, that's not what I –

SOPHIE: . . . a sub-human . . . let's see, what else . . .

MOHR: *(Quickly)* There's no need to be specific –

SOPHIE: . . . since you asked . . .

MOHR: *(Overriding her)* I am talking about the political implications of the ideas expressed.

SOPHIE: Politics? I don't know anything about politics.

MOHR: *(Looks at her for a moment)* No . . . *(Outside, the church bells toll the half hour)*

SOPHIE: Church bells, next door! I love them!

MOHR: They give me a headache.

THE WHITE ROSE

Resource sheet 8

Dramatic tension: a checklist

From the characters' point of view

What do they want to *achieve?*

- to succeed at a task?
- to gain power?
- to fall in love?
- to get out of a difficult situation?
- to make sense of what is happening to them?
- to seek revenge?
- to help someone?

What *pressures* are they under?

- the pressure of time?
- the pressure of competition?
- the pressure of the task?
- the pressure of responsibility?
- the pressure to make sense of what is happening?
- the pressure to make a choice?

What *constraints* affect them?

- constrained by space?
- constrained by relationships with others?
- constrained by a misunderstanding?
- constrained by lack of knowledge?
- constrained by personal inadequacy?
- constrained by conflict?
- constrained by protocol or ritual?
- constrained by an inability to make a decision?

From the audience's point of view

- How far do we identify with a character's situation?
- How far do we feel what they are feeling?
- Do we share their frustrations when things go wrong?
- Do we want to know what happens next?
- Are we surprised or shocked by what happens?
- Are we relieved when something finally happens?
- Do we 'know' something that a character does not?
- Is the fictional world depicted in the drama causing tension with something in our 'real life'?
- Are we excited by the performers' skill?

(adapted from Morgan and Saxton, 1987 and O'Toole and Haseman, 1988)

The Mysteries

Introduction and context

This unit can be used as a means of introducing the students to a specific style and form of theatre that has a didactic or moral learning element. Although there are many styles of theatre that fit into this category, the students exploring this unit will focus upon England's Medieval Mystery Cycle plays, commonly known as The Mysteries.

Within the study of any specific style or form there is, of course, a great deal of context to negotiate as the drama is placed within its social and historical context. Although some of this detail has been included, there is a choice to be made as to how much of this information is needed for the students to progress and get the most out of the work. Judicious teachers will be able to select the most important historical information needed for their groups, allowing the momentum of the drama work to take precedence and avoiding overwhelming the students with every last piece of contextual detail.

We encourage the sense of fun and enjoyment that the students can bring to this work. Enactments of the Mystery Cycle plays were celebratory, and during the in-role sections the students will respond to the friendly rivalry that can be set up between the guild groups. The element of acting on two levels – taking on the role of a guild member who is in turn taking on the role of a character in a play – offers a great deal of potential for comedy and satire, with clear links to contemporary and historical drama that can be followed up in later classes.

We anticipate that a group exploring all the activities in this unit would take about six one-hour lessons to complete the tasks.

Activity 1

Read one or two of the creation stories detailed on Resource sheet 1 (page 143), then ask the students to consider these questions:

- *What is the purpose of the story?*
- *Who is the story 'aimed at'?*
- *Who is telling the story?*

Explain that these stories are commonly called creation myths, but are more accurately referred to as creation *narratives* because, to the people that believe in them, these stories are considered to be true. Over thousands of years, these stories have endured as attempts to explain the creation of the world, define the origins of humankind and explain the natural order of people's lives within a particular culture or society. Creation narratives are truly global and predate fairytales and folklore, crossing cultures and times with their references and imagery.

Now ask the students to consider the word 'ritual'.

- What does this word mean to the group?
- Can they think of examples of rituals?
- What elements of language, movement or symbolism are commonly found in rituals?
- Can rituals be broken down into categories – religious, civil, formal and informal?

The *Mysteries* unit map

Activity	Description	Resources	Teacher notes
Activity 1	Creation stories; ritual performances.	Resource sheet 1, 2	
Activity 2	Introduction of the Mystery Cycle; heaven and hell *tableaux vivants*.	Resource sheet 3	
Activity 3	Assign 'guilds'; symbol and motto.	Resource sheet 4	
Activity 4	Master and apprentice.		
Activity 5	Teacher in role, meeting of guilds; 'auditions'.		
Activity 6	Script work; rehearsal.	Resource sheet 5, 6, 7, 8	
Activity 7	Performance and evaluation.		

A ritual can be defined as a series of actions that are performed or carried out according to the customs of a particular group, culture or society. A ritual could include movement and gesture, language or sounds, music, call and response, images and objects. Rituals rely on symbolism and metaphor to communicate meaning, and for those participating in the ritual it is often an affirming, transforming or celebratory experience. Rituals of this kind are described as having 'efficacy': they are examples of performance with a particular function or purpose within a particular group or society.

In groups of four or five, ask the students to devise a ritual based on a creation narrative selected from Resource sheet 1. This ritual could be framed as being the opening event in a ceremony celebrating their story. The performance should in some way communicate the essence, meaning or narrative of their assigned story. Encourage the groups to include the following elements into their ritual dramas:

- language – words, sentences or phrases from the text that could be uttered using direct address, narration, or choral speaking techniques of various kinds (see Resource sheet 2, page 144);
- symbolic or abstract movement – gesture, figurative mime ('body as props'); ensemble, cannon or repetitive effects.

Once the groups have had time to prepare their work, share the rituals.

- *Which of the ritualised performances were most effective? Why?*
- *Which of the rituals managed to communicate the narrative effectively?*
- *As an audience member, was it necessary for you to already know the story to make sense of the drama and the narrative itself?*

Activity 2

Explain that you are going to read out another creation narrative and ask the group if anyone recognises it:

> *In the beginning God created the heavens and the earth. Over seven days, God created light and called it day, and darkness which was called night. He separated the heaven from the earth and made the dry land and the seas. On the land, God put plants and in the heaven stars, the sun and moon. Then God created the diverse creatures that lived in the air, the sea and on dry land. Then came man and woman made in God's image. On the last day, God rested from his work.*

After identifying the story as that found in the Book of Genesis and belonging to the Judaeo-Christian faith, ask the class to identify any features in common with the creation narratives that they have just enacted.

Explain that the Mystery Cycles of medieval England used theatre to re-tell the stories of the Christian bible from Creation through to Judgement and in doing so, affirmed the religious and moral teaching elements found in the Bible. Resource sheet 3 (page 145) may help to build the students' contextual knowledge and introduce some key elements of this style of theatre – or you may wish to condense this information to suit the class.

The development of the Mystery Cycle

Elements of drama had become features of certain Christian church ceremonies and rituals in medieval times, yet the transition from this simple theatrical form to the sophistication and spectacle of the Mystery Cycle plays took time.

It is a matter of speculation as to how and why the dramas and drama rituals made their journey out of the church doors and into the places of performance in the towns. Perhaps the plays became too large for the church to accommodate, or it was considered inappropriate for members of the clergy to be seen acting in increasingly less formal circumstances.

In 1264 the Feast of Corpus Christi was introduced by Pope Urban and became a major celebration in the Christian calendar. By the early fourteenth century, the feast had become the focus for presenting the Mystery Cycles in many towns and cities across Britain.

It was the trade guilds and craft associations of the towns that assumed an increasingly important role in the production of the plays that made up the cycles. Specific guilds would take on the responsibility of staging and producing particular sections of the cycle. These guilds would provide costumes, props and sets that were designed on movable pageant wagons. There are a number of theories concerning the staging of the Mysteries:

1   Each guild would take part in a parade in which their pageant wagon, showing a tableau or still image from their play, was presented at different locations around the town. All the pageants were then located to a single performance area, possible around the town square, where the audience would sit on raised scaffolding surrounding the acting area.

---

continued

2 The pageant wagons were drawn to different stations along an accepted route where an audience would sit. The actors would stop, perform their play and then move on to the next location.

3 The performances happened outside town in a large circular area. The audience sat or stood within the 'round' as the action unfolded on static stages around the perimeter of the circle.

4 The pageants were placed in a long row, with each 'house' representing a different setting. The audience sat in front of this elongated stage.

The Mysteries represented something very important for the watching audience. It was a way of making real the tales of the Bible and making sure they were passed on to a largely illiterate audience.

These plays were performed in English and used local dialect and language that would be familiar to those watching. This, coupled with the use of trade and religious guild members and townsfolk to act out the various scenes, must have had a profound effect upon the audience. Here were people they knew, using familiar language to act out the stories that underpinned their religious beliefs. This must have been a strongly affirming experience that rooted the morals and teaching of Christianity into the everyday existence of the audience.

Two of the most important pageants were those that represented heaven and hell, and these featured tiers and balconies as well as winches and stage machinery. Often, hell was represented as an enormous pair of gaping jaws that spewed out smoke and fire and through which the actors could pass. For people who believed literally in the power of heaven and hell, to see these places represented on stage must have been a potent spectacle and a salutary reminder of the importance of following a 'good and proper' life. The fact that these plays were not performed in the formality of the church might also have symbolised how religion and religious teaching extended beyond the confines of the church walls, placing it in the streets and marketplaces of the ordinary people.

Explain that the next few tasks will be centred on exploring the historical importance of The Mysteries as a way of using drama to celebrate religious belief, learn about the Christian religious cycle and possibly affirm a moral or guiding influence upon their medieval audiences.

Introduce the idea that in medieval times the majority of the audience watching The Mysteries would have believed in the literal existence of heaven and hell. Now, ask the group to list words or phrases that they identify with the traditional or accepted concepts of heaven and hell. Explain that these representations were fundamental to the dramas and often framed the action of the plays in the cycle.

Divide the class into two and assign each group the task of creating a *tableau vivant* of heaven or hell. The first task of both groups is to create a tableau which represents their own concept of heaven or hell. Their second task is to divide this main image into a series of short animated sequences of movement and dialogue that could progress in a linear fashion from one end of the tableau to the other. The lists they have just composed should inform this task. As they work, the groups should consider what style of performance might be best utilised and may consider incorporating elements of ritual from the previous exercise.

Assign the groups different sides of the room to work in. When they have finished devising their drama, ask both groups to share their work facing each other.

- To make their drama more effective, what design or technical elements might help enhance the work?

- What style of drama worked best to communicate their intentions? Is humour or comedy an appropriate form to employ in this task?
- What mood or atmosphere were they attempting to communicate?
- Which of the presentations would be most powerful for an audience who believed that these visions of heaven and hell were literally true?

Activity 3

Explain that in medieval times it was the trade guilds that took responsibility for staging the plays in the cycle. A list of the plays and their respective guilds from the York cycle can be found on Resource sheet 4 (page 146) and this shows the range and scope of the plays as well as the variety of the guilds taking part. In some cases there are clear links between the subject matter of the play and the profession of the guilds, and in this way the staging of the plays would become an opportunity for the guilds to show the 'mastery' of their craft to a large audience.

> Medieval craft guilds became very important institutions that were designed to afford protection to both their members and the customers they served. Being a member of a craft guild was a prestigious position and allowed an individual to ply their trade or sell their products in their town. Skills were kept alive by ensuring that young apprentices were thoroughly trained by an older and more experienced guild member, a process that would often take years to complete. The guilds also set the prices the customers paid and they regulated their members, ensuring work was carried out to a high standard. This might include fining individuals, making them do a job again or even expelling them from the guild for poor workmanship. The guilds also raised money that could be used to support sick or older members and their families.

Place the students in groups of four or five and explain that, using Resource sheet 4, they must choose a guild from the list that will become their group identity for the rest of the work on this unit. Of course, many of the guilds represent professions that have now become extinct or so modernised that they bear little resemblance to their medieval beginnings. You may wish to assign each group a guild, perhaps using the less obscure and more easily understood professions.

Once each group of students is attached to a guild and understands the basic nature of their craft, explain that their first task is to design a coat of arms or crest that clearly identifies their guild and somehow signifies their 'mastery' of their occupation. As this image is to represent their group and their subsequent performance, it should be emphasised that only the highest quality design can be accepted. Along with an image or symbol, the groups should compose an accompanying motto or slogan. This task could be completed on sugar paper with colour markers, or designed on computer and printed out and enlarged.

Activity 4

With each guild's image or crest displayed in their working area, ask each of the students to get into pairs within their guild group. Explain that the next exercise is called Master and Apprentice. One student takes the role of the master craftsman and develops a detailed mime showing his or her interpretation of their skill or trade. They must then teach this to their apprentice, who must accurately learn the movements. The exercise is only complete when the master is completely satisfied that the apprentice has applied themselves diligently to the task and learnt the movements precisely.

After sharing one or two examples, ask the guilds to reform again. Their new task is to identify the best sequences of movement from all the pairs and create a piece of physical theatre that represents their guild's work. One aspect from each of the pairs must be incorporated into the final performance.

The groups might consider adding words, sounds or percussive noises and explore different ways of presenting the sequence of movements – perhaps using ensemble or cannoning one movement into the next as a chain or production line. Once the groups have had sufficient time to prepare, share the work.

As an extension to this task and to introduce a sense of rivalry between the guilds, assign each guild their neighbouring group's work to parody or satirise. In this way the coopers could poke fun at the tanners or the nail makers could 'send up' the scriveners. Framing this exercise as being slightly less serious and more 'tongue-in-cheek' encourages an irreverent, fun aspect to the work and neatly leads into the next phase of the role work by establishing a sense of friendly rivalry.

Activity 5

Explain that the work will now progress with the whole group in role and that you intend to take the role of the cleric responsible for staging the town's version of the Mysteries. The group is to imagine life in England 500 years ago and invent a name for their town.

- *What does our town look like?*
- *Is it a remote town or does it share close neighbours?*
- *What do the buildings look like?*
- *What are the roads and thoroughfares like?*
- *Are there any special features that make our town different?*

A meeting has been called to discuss arrangements for the forthcoming festival. There is certainly scope to make this work lighthearted and this could start with building a sense of competition between the guilds or perhaps with a neighbouring town. Hints that their particular town or guild is less than well organised – or perhaps has a history of previous theatrical disasters to its credit – might also steer the students towards the idea that the guild members were not professional actors.

The students will have to remember that they are acting on two 'levels': they are taking on the role of a guild member who is also presenting a character in a performance. A modern day parallel might be a local amateur dramatic group who meet once a week to rehearse for a performance in their village hall. As the students consider this, ask them to think about how they would portray their character in the play script if their guild role:

- thinks they are excellent at acting – when in reality they always overact;
- is extremely shy and does not like being the centre of attention with a main part;
- always gets their lines, entrances and exits mixed up;
- is very bossy and wants to lead the group all the time.

Shakespeare offers a satirical view of what a rehearsal of such a group of actors might look like in his comedy *A Midsummer Night's Dream*. A group of artisans known as the Mechanicals meets to rehearse a play to be performed at the wedding of the Duke and Duchess. Under the direction of Quince, this company of amateur actors prepares their version of 'The most Lamentable Comedy and most Cruel Death of Pyramus and Thisby.' You may wish to read out or allow the students to explore Act 1 scene II (Quince assigning parts to the company), Act 3 scene I (the first rehearsal) or Act 5 scene I (the performance).

Introduce the next section in role:

> *Kindly listen. As you know, our preparations for our town's Mystery Plays have begun. The guilds present here are those who have been chosen to perform some of the most important scenes. I need not remind you of what happened last time . . . but luckily the roof of the town hall has been mended and nearly all of the Bishop's hair has grown back – so no more fire spewing from the Mouth of Hell please . . .*

We all know that each guild here thinks that they are the best. But last time, the competition was ridiculous. So, before you are given your parts to act out, each guild is to audition and the best guild's work will be chosen for the most prestigious plays.

Either in or out of role, go on to explain that the guilds will have a limited amount of time to prepare a short drama that shows why their group is best suited to performing in the play. The drama could include:

- 'examples' of previous performances;
- a song, chant or dance;
- 'proof' that they have the best actors by showing short audition speeches. These could be clowns performing a comic routine or *lazzi*, or a speech in the best tragic tradition;
- jibes or pointed remarks that highlight the weaknesses of the other guilds.

When the groups are ready to perform, set up the auditions in role as the cleric. A suitably 'serious' – but perhaps tongue in cheek – delivery may lend a sense of importance to the proceedings.

At the end of the performances comments are invited from the audience and, in role as the cleric, the teacher should sum up the endeavours of the guilds and explain that the guilds may now pass on to the actual rehearsal of the play scripts.

Activity 6

The concluding script activities for this unit can be interpreted in a number of ways. Four complete scripts are provided for the guilds to perform (Resource sheets 5 to 8, pages 145–57); however, time constraints might mean that to rehearse and perform these in their entirety is impractical. In this case the guild groups could therefore:

- divide up the scripts into sections and perform some selected passages;
- present a drama showing the guild members actually rehearsing for their performance. This work could lead effectively into a comparison with The Mechanicals in *A Midsummer Night's Dream*.

However, if the desired conclusion to the unit is for the group to present a mini-cycle of Mystery Plays, the following approach could be followed.

The students will be given the script of a play adapted from a medieval original. They are to read through the text, cast the actors, rehearse and finally perform as part of a 'mini-cycle' that involves the whole group. One member of each group should take on the role of the director. As the only non-actor in the group, their task is to oversee the style and interpretation of the performance, as well as focusing upon individual performers and their characterisations. They should attempt to decode the author's overall intention by interpreting stage directions, the language and any subtext. They may need to include movement and business not specified directly, but inferred or alluded to in the text. The plays are *Adam and Eve*, *The Flood*, *The Second Shepherd's Play* and *The Crucifixion*.

The groups also have the option to explore further the 'two-tier' acting possibilities, and this would certainly influence their final performance.

Once the students are working on these modernised versions, remind the directors of some of the stylistic conventions that should influence their group's performance. Referring to Resource sheets 2 and 3 may help the directors define some of these elements. Considering acting style, ask the directors to consider:

- the subject matter, and how it is treated by the playwright, often to comic effect;
- how they choose to represent their characters;
- how performing outdoors might affect the style of delivery and presentation;

- the nature and size of the audience;
- the scale of the complete cycle;
- the fact that the dialogue was written in verse, featured dialect words and phrases and was performed in the local accent.

At this stage, the groups will also need to identify the way the performances will be staged. The directors must agree on one of the following conventions for the staging of the mini-cycle:

- A performance space is designated that is used by each group in turn. The action could be end-on, in the round or traverse (the performance takes place in the corridor between two groups of spectators facing each other).
- Each group remains in their designated space, turning the action of their play towards the centre of the room and the assembled audience. Spectators remain in their space, or stand and surround the action – promenade style – of the performing group.
- Each group takes their position in a line and the performances take place one after the other.
- The audience remains static and the performing groups travel, in sequence.

As these plays are fairly substantial, the groups will need sufficient time to develop their work to an acceptable performance standard. During the rehearsals, encourage them to review their performance and audit which elements of this very specific theatre form they have managed to incorporate into their work.

Activity 7

Share the work, employing the agreed staging conventions. Once the performances have been completed, review the whole task by considering the success of each group's performance within the context of the whole group's presentation.

- What particular challenges were presented by staging the different scripts?
- Were the groups pleased with their interpretation of their script?
- What conclusions have the groups made about the acting style that might have been adopted by the actors in medieval times?
- As a member of the audience, did the plays communicate effectively? Would there be a different experience for a medieval audience compared to that of a contemporary audience?
- What design elements might have enhanced their performances – costumes, mask, make-up, props, lighting, sound, or music?
- Are these design elements necessary to communicate the essence of these stories?

As a further activity, the groups may benefit from comparing the simpler, modernised version they have just performed with an example of an original script.

The class could also research those towns that still stage parts of The Mysteries. The cities of Chester and York in the UK still regularly perform parts of their cycles using professional and amateur actors. Images, descriptions and reviews of these performances can be found on the Internet.

THE MYSTERIES

Resource sheet 1: world creation narratives

Phan Ku (Chinese)

Before Phan Ku, all was chaos and darkness. From the darkness formed the universe, in the shape of a hen's egg, and inside the egg grew Phan Ku, the First Being, the Creator of All Things.

Phan Ku grew to the size of a giant, until he stretched and broke the egg. Horns grew out of his head, and huge tusks from his jaw. As the lighter parts of the egg floated upwards they formed the heavens – the Yin. The heavier parts sank downwards to form the earth – the Yang. In his hand Phan Ku held a chisel, and with it he carved out the world. With his chisel, Phan Ku carved out the rivers and valleys and mountains of the earth and he placed the sun, stars and moon in the sky.

To stop the earth and heavens becoming one again, Phan Ku held the heavens up with his head with his feet braced against the earth. Like this, Phan Ku grew for thousands of years until the gulf between earth and stars was immense. Exhausted from his trials, Phan Ku fell asleep, never to waken.

Phan Ku's dead body became the world. Rivers and seas were formed from his blood, soil from his body, and rocks from his bones. All the plants of the earth grew from Phan Ku's hair. Rain was made from his sweat. The wind is his breath, thunder and lightning the sound of his voice. From the fleas that lived on his hairy body came all of humankind.

Pandora (Greek)

The Gods in heaven created Pandora. Before she left heaven, she was given a box to keep from Zeus. She was told never to open it. Pandora puzzled over the box and what might be inside, but dared not look in it. Pandora was sent to Epimetheus who had helped fashion the men and animals of the earth. He instantly fell in love with her.

Epimetheus was suspicious of the box, having been told of Zeus' tricks, and hid the box high on a shelf. When his brother Prometheus returned, he was angry to find Pandora and told his brother he should never have accepted a gift from Zeus. Meanwhile Pandora continued to puzzle over the box, eventually finding it high on the shelf where her husband had put it. Reaching up, she slipped and the box tumbled to the floor, opening as it went. From the box came a great sound and all the surprises Zeus had put in it came tumbling out – hunger, poverty, pain, envy and despair and all the sorrowful things that would plague humans forever. As these creatures slithered, crept and crawled out into the world one last creature was left; it was Hope, who followed the ugly things and gave hope to all.

Ulgen the Creator (Russian)

In the mud of the waters, the God Ulgen saw a human face. He shaped it into the first man, who he named Erlik, and they became friends. As time went on Erlik started to boast that he could create life, just as Ulgen had done. Angry with him, Ulgen cast him down into the depths and Erlik became the devil.

Next, Ulgen created the earth. He planted seven trees and planted a man under each tree. He also made a golden mountain and placed on it an eighth tree. Under this tree he put the eighth man – Maidere. But although the trees grew branches, the men did not change. Maidere told Ulgen that the men could not change, as there were no womenfolk for them. Ulgen commanded Maidere to make women.

Maidere created the first woman, but could not give her life. He sought Ulgen for help, leaving Woman guarded by Dog. But Erlik came when Maidere had left and tricked Dog by promising him a fur coat to keep him warm. Erlick gave the woman life by playing music – seven notes on a flute and nine on a harp – but also gave her seven tempers and nine moods. As punishment for not guarding Woman better, Maidere cursed Dog, and commanded that Dog's fur coat would continue to grow forever.

THE MYSTERIES

Resource sheet 2

Choral techniques

1   Simple choral speaking in unison.

2   Break the text/into sections/and give each student/or group of students/a section to speak/
     either unison/or solo.

3   Break the text into single words and allocate them to students. Speak the text a

    Word
        at
          a
           time!

4   Break the text down even further: each word in-to syll-a-bles.

5   Echo
    Echo
       Echo . . .   (overlapping)

6   Echo
      Echo
          Echo . . .   (with pause between)

7   Repeat sections of the textofthetextrepeatsectionsofthetext . . .

               a
8   Use onomatopoeia: f l o t, **HEAVY**, *burst!*, sizzzzzzzzzzle, etc.

9   Experiment   with   **dynamics!**

10   Experiment with expression: tone; timbre; musicality; whispers; singing; chanting; deadpan,
      etc.

11   Use combinations of the above . . . carefully choreographed, of course.

12   . . . and any other techniques you can think of!

THE MYSTERIES

Resource sheet 3

A guide to medieval Mystery Cycle plays

- The term Mystery play is understood to come from the Latin word *mysterium*, which means trade or handicraft.
- The Mystery Cycle plays are made up of re-enactments of bible stories and episodes that tell the story of the birth, betrayal, death and resurrection of Christ and can be divided into The Creation, Passion and Doomsday.
- Each play in the cycle was performed by a religious or trade guild that was responsible for that particular story, on or around the time of the Feast of Corpus Christi. Sometimes there was a link between the trade and the plays they were responsible for.
- There are a number of ideas concerning the staging of the Mysteries:

  1   Each guild would take part in a parade in which their pageant wagon, showing a tableau or still image from their play, was presented at different locations around the town. All the pageants were then located to a single performance area, possible around the town square, where the audience would sit on raised scaffolding surrounding the acting space.

  2   The pageant wagons were drawn to different stations along an accepted route where an audience would sit. The actors would stop, perform their play and then move on to the next location.

  3   The performances happened outside town in a large circular area. The audience sat or stood within the 'round' as the action unfolded on static stages around the perimeter of the circle.

  4   The pageants were placed in a long row, with each 'house' representing a different setting. The audience sat in front of this elongated stage.

- A number of 'cycles' still exist from Chester, York, Wakefield and the ambiguous 'N-Town'. Many more towns and cities would have had their own cycle. Some cities still regularly present a cycle of Mystery Plays, featuring local amateur and professional actors.
- The language was in verse and featured local words and dialects familiar to the audience.
- The actors would have to cope with performing outside to very large and possibly noisy audiences, who might be at a considerable distance from the action.
- Music and songs were incorporated into the plays.
- Many of the pageant wagons featured elaborate staging that included machinery to animate clouds or waves, lift actors or create smoke or fire. Dramatic sound effects, fireworks and even the use of water would have made for quite impressive performances.

THE MYSTERIES

Resource sheet 4

The full list of plays and their associated guilds, York Cycle

1 The Creation, and the Fall of Lucifer (Barkers).
2 The Creation – up to the Fifth Day (Plasterers).
3 Creation of Adam and Eve (Cardmakers).
4 Adam and Eve in Eden (Fullers).
5 Fall of Man (Coopers).
6 Expulsion from Eden (Armourers).
7 Sacrifice of Cain and Able (Glovers).
8 Building of the Ark (Shipwrights).
9 Noah and his Wife; Flood (Fishers and Mariners).
10 Abraham and Isaac (Parchmenters and Bookbinders).
11 Departure of the Israelites from Egypt; Ten Plagues; Crossing of the Red Sea (Hosiers).
12 Annunciation and Visitation (Spicers).
13 Joseph's Trouble about Mary (Pewterers and Founders).
14 Journey to Bethlehem; Birth of Jesus (Tile-thatchers).
15 Shepherds (Chandlers).
16 Coming of the Three Kings to Herod (Masons).
17 Coming of the Kings; Adoration (Goldsmiths).
18 Flight into Egypt (Marshalls).
19 Slaughter of the Innocents (Girdlers and Nailers).
20 Christ with the Doctors (Spurriers and Lorimers).
21 Baptism of Jesus (Barbers).
22 Temptation (Smiths).
23 Transfiguration (Curriers).
24 Woman Taken in Adultery; Lazarus (Capmakers).
25 Christ's Entry into Jerusalem (Skinners).
26 Conspiracy (Cutlers).
27 Last Supper (Bakers).
28 Agony and Betrayal (Cordwainers).
29 Peter's Denial; Jesus before Caiaphas (Bowyers and Fletchers).
30 Dream of Pilate's Wife; Jesus before Pilate (Tapiters and Couchers).
31 Trial before Herod (Listers).
32 Second Accusation before Pilate; Remorse of Judas; Purchase of the Field of Blood (Cooks and Water-leaders).
33 Second Trial before Pilate (Tilemakers).
34 Christ Led to Calvary (Shearmen).
35 Crucifixion (Pinners and Painters).
36 Mortification of Christ; Burial (Butchers).
37 Harrowing of Hell (Saddlers).
38 Resurrection (Carpenters).
39 Christ's Appearance to Mary Magdalene (Winedrawers).
40 Travellers to Emmaus (Sledmen).
41 Purification of Mary; Simeon and Anna (Hatmakers, Masons, Labourers).
42 Incredulity of Thomas (Scriveners).
43 Ascension (Tailors).
44 Descent of the Holy Spirit (Potters).
45 Death of Mary (Drapers).
46 Appearance of Mary to Thomas (Weavers).
47 Assumption and Coronation of the Virgin (Hostlers).
48 Judgement (Mercers).

THE MYSTERIES

Resource sheet 5

Adam and Eve *from* Original Sin *by Peter Leach*

Characters:
Adam, Eve, Satan, God.

The play takes place in the Garden of Eden.

> [*Satan appears and addresses the audience.*]

SATAN: A Paradise for Man!
               And we, who once were Angels bright,
               Must suffer in the fires of Hell
               For all Eternity!

               Very well! It shall be my delight
               To spoil his plan.
               I'll make Him wish he never made Man!

               I'll teach Mankind to disobey and fall from grace.
               I'll lead him into Sin with wicked lies
               And with Woman I'll begin

               [*Calling to EVE*] Eve! Eve!

EVE: Who are you?
SATAN: A friend would you believe.
               Tell me is it true,
               You must not eat any fruit in Paradise?
EVE: We can eat anything!
SATAN: Can you?
EVE: Anything we find that's nice,
               Except the fruit on that tree.
SATAN: Who gave you that advice?
EVE: God, He forbids us, Adam and me.
               If we did we'd pay the price and Paradise
               We'd have to leave.
SATAN: Eve! God has told you a lie!
               That's what he wants you to believe.
               He told you that to stop you having the power
               You'd receive if you ate that fruit.
               It's true! That fruit brings knowledge
               Of good and evil.
EVE: Why should I believe you?
SATAN: I'm a friend.
               Take my advice then you'll have a life
               Of bliss.
EVE: No! We're happy here, Adam and me.
               It's nice. We don't need that fruit.
SATAN: Listen to me!
               You think that Paradise is enough!
               You could be Gods yourselves!
               Equal to him! Greater yet!

EVE: Is that the truth?

SATAN: Can't you see! You will be worshipped!

[*Satan tempts Eve to eat the Forbidden Fruit.*]

SATAN: Eat the fruit of the tree, there is no danger.
Eat!

EVE: I will! [*EVE stretches out to take the apple.*]

SATAN: And Adam too.

EVE: Yes! [*EVE plucks the apple from the tree.*]

SATAN: Take a bite, it's sweet.

EVE: Yes! [*EVE takes a single bite.*]

SATAN: Good. Now I'll leave you. [*SATAN steps aside and retires upstage where he remains, watching the action as if hiding. EVE continues to eat the apple.*]

[*Adam walks forward.*]

EVE: Adam!

ADAM: The tree!

EVE: Eat this!

ADAM: You knew we mustn't touch it
When He . . . When He finds out!

EVE: [*Shouts.*] ADAM! Listen to me!

ADAM: SSSH! Keep your voice down. Don't shout.

EVE: Adam, if we eat this – we shall be Gods!
One bite will make us as wise as He.

ADAM: [*Looking around him.*] Well . . . I don't know . . . I might . . . if it's true.

EVE: We'll be as wise as God himself. We'll have power!

ADAM: Alright! Give it to me. [*He snatches the apple and eats.*]
Pah . . . Ugh . . . It's sour!
What have I done?
You're to blame!

EVE: Oh! Oh Adam.

[*SATAN appears from his hiding place.*]

SATAN: Now for some fun!

ADAM: [*ADAM suddenly realises they are both naked.*] We're naked! We're both undone!
We've sinned! It was you!
You've brought us to this shame!
What shall we do?

EVE: It's not my fault, he made me do it!
I didn't want to!

SATAN: Too late!

ADAM: We must hide . . . cover our shame . . . God mustn't see. [*Searches for something to hide behind.*] Take this leaf.

EVE: He made me . . . he's to blame!

[*God appears.*]

GOD: ADAM! ADAM!

ADAM: Lord, we . . .

GOD: What have you done?

ADAM: It's not my fault, Eve made me.

EVE: I'm not to blame. [*Pointing to SATAN*] He's the one,
He tempted me.

GOD: [*God turns to SATAN.*] SATAN!

SATAN: Me again!

GOD: Satan I curse you to everlasting pain,
On your belly you shall creep . . . Go! [*SATAN exits crawling.*]
Adam and Eve into the rain and cold I banish you,
You shall toil and weep on Earth.
In the garden, you can no longer stay.
Go now, in sorrow. [*ADAM and EVE exit.*]
Paradise is lost today.

THE MYSTERIES

Resource sheet 6

The Flood *from* Original Sin *by Peter Leach*

Characters:
God, Noah, Noah's Wife, Neighbour, Noah's son Shem.

[*Spoken or sung directly to the audience.*]

GOD: Things haven't gone according to my plan
Now I wish that I'd never made Man.
See the state the world is in.
Full of violence, full of sin.
The Devil grins and causes me much pain,
I've decided I'm going to start again.

I'll bring the Flood on the face of the land.
I'll wash it clean with the power of my hand.
I'll send destruction and bring the rain clouds down.
Hear my voice in the thunder
Watch the whole world drown.

[*As God has been speaking, NOAH has appeared.*]

GOD: All of you sitting there,
Not one of you will I spare!
Only Noah. Noah!
NOAH: Yes, Lord?
GOD: Noah, you have listened to my song,
You have noticed something's wrong.
You alone will I save.
In an Ark, you will escape a watery grave.
NOAH: Lord, I'll hurry home and tell the wife,
But she's bound to moan,
It's always the same.
Day in, day out – trouble and strife!
She'll nag and shout and say I'm to blame.
Her temper's bad. The least little thing makes her mad.
WIFE: NOAH!
NOAH: Oh dear, she's coming.
WIFE: NOAH!
NOAH: Hello dear . . .
WIFE: Oh, you're there. [*Suspiciously.*] Where have you been?
I've looked high and low, you just disappear –
to God knows where! Not that I care –
You ought to know – I've enough to do,
The dinner to cook, without having to come and look
For you!
NOAH: Yes . . . but listen dear . . . I've something important to say . . .
WIFE: He's never here – no consideration!
Too busy preaching The Word. He's at it every day.
People think that you're absurd, going on about salvation.
It gives me a pain!

NOAH: But the end of the world IS nigh!
             Look at the sky!
             It's going to rain.
WIFE: Don't be silly!
NOAH: God said!
WIFE: Oh, been talking to Him again have you?
             I sometimes think he's not right in the head.
NOAH: I've got to build a boat.
WIFE: A what?
NOAH: A boat – He told me.
WIFE: He is insane!
NOAH: And when this is all sea, we'll be able to float.
WIFE: He's getting too old.
             Well, I'm off home, you can stay on your own,
             But your dinner's cold! [*NOAH's WIFE exits.*]
NOAH: Thank God she's gone! Now I can get on
             And build the boat.
             I'm not much of a carpenter, I hope it'll float.

[*NOAH starts to build the boat.*]

This is hard work, I'll have to take off my coat.

[*NOAH's WIFE, SHEM their son and a NEIGHBOUR come to watch.*]

NEIGHBOUR: Well, I'd never have believed it!
WIFE: I told you . . . he's insane.
NEIGHBOUR: What's he making it for?
WIFE: He says God told him it's going to rain.
NOAH: My back is sore.
             Now let's see, according to the plan it ought to be,
             Yes! Three hundred cubits exactly.
NEIGHBOUR: I've never seen such a sight!
NOAH: And the height . . . fifty cubits, it's going well,
             And thirty wide . . .
NEIGHBOUR: What is it?
WIFE: It's an ARK, can't you tell?
NEIGHBOUR: But what is he going to put inside?
NOAH: Now for the mast.
NEIGHBOUR: Was that a spot of rain?
NOAH: There, finished at last and just in time,
             The sky's getting dark.
NEIGHBOUR: I'll have to go, I've left my washing out. [*The NEIGHBOUR exits.*]
NOAH: Right – I must get the family inside the Ark. Shem!
SHEM: Yes dad?
NOAH: Do as I say, fetch the animals – two by two.
             Hurry!
WIFE: He is mad! He's built a bloody zoo!

[*There is the sound of thunder.*]

NOAH: Now then wife, you hear that thunder?
             Very soon the world will drown.
             Everywhere will be under water, so hurry!
             Get ready.
WIFE: I'm not leaving this town.

NOAH: Wife, why don't you understand?
           God is going to destroy the land. Come in!
WIFE: No! I shall sit here and knit.
SON: It's raining hard.
NOAH: You can knit inside.
SON: It's getting worse.
NOAH: Don't be perverse.
WIFE: Well . . . I am getting wet. Perhaps it would be best.
NOAH: At last. She's seen sense! COME IN!
WIFE: Don't you shout at me, Noah.
NOAH: Stubborn yet! I'll knock some sense into you!
WIFE: Just you try and see what you get.
NOAH: You'll feel my fist!
WIFE: I'm a match for you!
NOAH: Right, you asked for it!
WIFE: You'll have to catch me first, you silly old . . .

           [*Thunder drowns her final insult. The slapstick chase and fight mirror the building
           storm.*]

NOAH: Enough . . . no more . . . I'm black and blue.
SON: You ought to be ashamed, the pair of you.
           Quick, come inside.
NOAH: Come on wife, come in.
WIFE: NO!
SON: Mother!
WIFE: I'm not taking orders from him.
SON: Mother, come in!
NOAH: YOU CAN'T SWIM!

           [*The storm reaches its climax. Suddenly it stops. Their heads appear over the edge
           of the Ark.*]

NOAH: It's stopped. It's stopped.
           Forty days and forty nights have passed.
           The rain has stopped at last.
           A raven will I send and if this bird does not return
           It is a sign that the flood is at an end. [*NOAH throws the bird into the sky. The
           family follows the bird's flight with their eyes until it disappears into the distance.*]
           Somewhere is dry, I see.
           The raven does not return to me.
           Now a dove will I send.
           He will return. [*Again Noah launches a bird into flight and the family follows
           its journey, this time the bird returns, landing back in NOAH's cupped hands.*]
           See! A sign!
           The dove has brought an olive branch from some place.
           It is a token of God's grace, a sign of peace.

           [*God appears.*]

GOD: NOAH!
           I have caused the flood to cease.
           The earth is dry.
           Now in the sky, you see my bow.
           By this token you may know that never again
           Will I destroy the earth with rain.
           Now, go forth, and start again.

           [*NOAH and family exit.*]

THE MYSTERIES

Resource sheet 7

Mak the Sheep Stealer (The Second Shepherd's Play)
from **Original Sin** *by Peter Leach*

Characters:
Angel, First Shepherd, Second Shepherd, Mak the sheep stealer, Gill his wife.

The action takes place in two locations: on the heath with the shepherds and their flock, and in Mak and Gill's house.

[*An Angel appears and speaks directly to the audience.*]

ANGEL: And there were, in the same country,
Shepherds abiding in the fields.
Keeping watch over their flock by night.

[*Enter the shepherds. There is the noise of sheep.*]

FIRST: What a life!
SHEEP: BAA.
FIRST: I've never known it so cold.
SHEEP: BAA.
SECOND: Looks like snow.
FIRST: That's all we need.
    Right, count the flock.
SECOND: What?
FIRST: Do as you're told – count the sheep!
SECOND: Oh, all right. [*Begins to count.*]
    Yahn . . . Tayn . . . Tether . . . Mether . . . Mumph . . .
    Hither . . . Lither . . . Auver . . . Dauver . . . Dic . . .
    Yahndic . . . Tayndic . . . Tetherdic . . . Metherdic . . . Mumphit . . .
    Yahn-a-mumphit . . . Tayn-a-mumphit . . . Thethera-mumphit . . .
    Methera-mumphit . . . Jig-it.
    All there!
FIRST: Right.
SECOND: Counting sheep always makes me sleepy. [*He yawns.*]
FIRST: Me too.
SECOND: What about the flock?
FIRST: Oh, they'll be alright. They'll come to no harm,
    If anything happens, they'll give the alarm.
SHEEP: BAA.
FIRST: Goodnight. [*They both fall asleep, snoring noisily.*]

[*Mak enters, carrying an empty sack.*]

MAK: Bloody weather! It's getting worse.
I've never known it so cold.
My fingers are numb.
And look at this coat,
It's old and full of holes.
It don't keep out the wind and rain.
Aye, it's alright for some.
And Gill – the wife – she's been ill again.
She's had another, but what can you do?

> She just swells up, regular as clockwork
> And then – pop – out comes another one,
> Sometimes two!
> We've a house full of kids.
> But she's a wonderful mother.
> Aye, times are hard, we can't make ends meet.
> Still, I can't stand here talking to you.
> My shoes are freezing to my feet,
> And we need something to eat.
> So . . .
> While they sleep . . .
> I'll just creep . . .
> Up to the flock . . .
> And borrow a sheep.
> GOTCHA!
> Right – I'm off home.
> He's nice and fat!
> Lamb chops and stew!
> I can't wait to get my teeth into you!

[*The sheep begin to raise the alarm.*]

FIRST:	What's the matter?
	What's all the fuss?
SECOND:	On my back! I can't move!
	Help me up!
FIRST:	Flipping heck!
SECOND:	I must have laid all wrong,
	I've got a stiff neck.
FIRST:	What's wrong with the sheep?
SECOND:	I don't know, I was asleep.
FIRST:	Something's wrong,
	We'd better check.

[*The action shifts to MAK and GILL's house.*]

MAK:	Quick Gill, let me in!
GILL:	Stop that din! Who is it?
MAK:	Me, of course.
GILL:	Who?
MAK:	Me! Mak! Let me in!
	I can't stand out here all night.
GILL:	Alright . . . alright, [*She opens the door.*]
	I'd just got to sleep.
	Here, what's in the sack?
MAK:	Look! A sheep.
GILL:	A sheep?
	And where do you think we're going to keep that?
	I'm not having it in my house, getting under my feet.
MAK:	It's not a pet, you stupid . . . it's dinner!
	It's to eat.
GILL:	Well I'm not going to start cooking at this time of night.
MAK:	But the shepherds will come looking.
	When they count the flock and find one missing
	They're bound to come here, they always do.

GILL:	Well you shouldn't keep stealing their sheep.
MAK:	Oh shut up, and let me think!
	We need somewhere to hide this lamb.
GILL:	I've got an idea.
MAK:	You?
GILL:	We'll put him in the pram.
MAK:	Brilliant!
	Wrap him up well, no-one will be able to tell.
GILL:	Get him inside . . .
MAK:	Here, there's a funny smell.

[*On the heath.*]

FIRST:	[*Counting the sheep.*] Yahn-a-mumphit . . . Tayn-a-mumphit . . . Thethera-mumphit . . . Methera-mumphit . . . Jig-it. ONE GONE!
SECOND:	Are you sure?
FIRST:	Yes, I've counted them twice.
	We've lost a sheep.
SECOND:	You shouldn't have gone to sleep.
FIRST:	Me? What about you?
	Oh, never mind.
	We'll have to find it, it can't have gone far.
	Search over there, I'll look around here.
SECOND:	Here's a clue.
	In the snow – footprints.
FIRST:	Right, let's follow and see where they take us to.

[*MAK and GILL's house.*]

MAK:	Quick Gill, I think they're coming.

[*MAK and GILL pretend to comfort the 'baby' and sing a lullaby.*]

FIRST:	I might have known,
	The footprints lead straight back to Mak.
SECOND:	What a din.
FIRST:	You knock.
SECOND:	Mak, are you in?
MAK:	Go away, the baby's asleep.
SECOND:	We want a word with you.
FIRST:	We've lost a sheep.
	You wouldn't know anything about it, I suppose?
MAK:	Me? A sheep? No!
	Look, it's the middle of the night.
	Come back tomorrow, we've enough sorrow.
FIRST:	We're coming in.
GILL:	Shut yer row! Stop that bloody din!
	You can't come in, I'm in bed.
MAK:	There's no sheep here.
FIRST:	We'll just make sure.
GILL:	Get out! Help! Show some respect!
MAK:	Can't you see, she's not well.
SECOND:	What's that funny smell?
MAK:	Please, we don't have your sheep.
FIRST:	Well, if it wasn't you,
	Then who was it came through the snow,
	And left a trail from the flock to your door?

MAK:	Ah . . . come to think of it, there was a knock,
	About eleven o'clock. But we didn't look
	To see who, must have been someone passing through.
FIRST:	Is that true? [*To SECOND SHEPHERD.*] What do you think?
SECOND:	I don't know.
	[*Sniffing the air loudly.*] Here, here's a terrible stink!
GILL:	No, go away before you wake the kids.
	Go on, keep away from the pram!
	Don't you dare go near, he's asleep, the little lamb!
FIRST:	We've made a mistake.
	Mak, I hope you won't take offence.
	We were wrong, we're sorry.
SECOND:	[*Still sniffing.*] There's an awful pong!
FIRST:	We'd best get along, but before we go, here's
	A little gift for the boy, [*Reaches into his pocket and gives MAK a coin.*]
	Buy him a present.
SECOND:	Get him a toy.
MAK:	Yes, thanks very much.
	Now will you go, we need our sleep.
SECOND:	Can I just take a peep?
GILL:	NO!
FIRST:	Oh, come on Mak. Let's see the lad.
GILL:	Oh, my head, I'm feeling bad!
SECOND:	I only want to give him a little kiss.
MAK:	No, you can't do this.
FIRST:	I'll lift him out. [*Reaches into the pram and lifts out the sheep, cradling it like a baby.*]
MAK:	Oh no!
SECOND:	Oh!
FIRST:	He's got a long snout.
GILL:	You'll make him cry.
SECOND:	Here, just like our sheep.
GILL:	He's a pretty little thing,
	A proper little lamb.
FIRST:	Who's the father?
MAK:	I am.
SECOND:	Look, that's our mark on his ear.
MAK:	He just looks a bit queer,
	Because his nose is broken.
	He was bewitched by an elf in the night –
	I saw it myself – when he was asleep.
FIRST & SECOND:	[*Together.*] It's our bloody sheep.
MAK:	Quick Gill, run.
FIRST:	Come back here you two!
SECOND:	I'll beat him black and blue!
FIRST:	We'll teach you to steal our sheep!

[*The shepherds chase and catch MAK and GILL.*]

FIRST:	Grab him!
SECOND:	Right, I'll black his eyes and punch his nose.

[*There is a scuffle. The fight freezes as the Angel appears.*]

ANGEL:	Shepherds arise.
	Peace on earth.
	Goodwill to all men.
MAK:	Hark, do you hear?
	Voices in the sky.
	Angels calling from on high.
GILL:	Now see what you've done.
	You've hit him so hard, his sense has gone.
	He's hearing things.
ANGEL:	I bring glad tidings
	To you and all mankind.
FIRST:	I can hear them as well.
SECOND:	And look, that star so bright.
GILL:	Mak, I'm scared!
	I'm full of fright.
ANGEL:	Fear not.
	For now He is born,
	In Bethlehem upon this morn,
	The Saviour – Christ the Lord.

[*The Angel fades away.*]

MAK:	Did you hear?
	Did you see?
GILL:	Yes, I did.
FIRST & SECOND:	[*Together.*] So did we.
GILL:	Mak, we must go and see this baby.
MAK:	No, we can't, not you and me.
GILL:	Why not?
MAK:	We're sinners, aren't we?
	How can we go and pay a visit?
FIRST:	It's sinners that he's come to save.
MAK:	Is it?
SECOND:	Yes, that's what the prophets tell.
MAK:	Well, in that case, you can come as well!

[*The whole group exits.*]

THE MYSTERIES

Resource sheet 8

The Crucifixion *by Peter Leach*

Characters:
First Soldier, Second Soldier, Third Soldier, Jesus.

The action takes place on Calvary Hill.

FIRST:	This one's Jesus Christ.
SECOND:	Poor sod.
FIRST:	Calls himself the son of God!
THIRD:	Now come on lads, don't delay –
	He must be dead by noon today.
SECOND:	Let's bash his brains out . . .
FIRST:	Yeah, that's best.
THIRD:	No. We'll crucify him, like the rest.
	You fetch the ropes.
FIRST:	Hammers too – and nails,
	Six inch'll do.
THIRD:	Set the cross down on the ground.
SECOND:	We'll soon have you up safe and sound.
JESUS:	Forgive them, father
	For they know not what they do.
FIRST:	Did you hear that! Did you?
	Shut yer mouth you bloody Jew!
SECOND:	Here, King of the Jews – a crown!
FIRST:	Now – on the cross – get down!
THIRD:	You take his right hand,
	You grab his feet.
SECOND:	We'll soon have you fixed up a treat!
THIRD:	Right – pull on his arm.
	Pass the pin. [*He begins to hammer in the first nail.*]
	That's one nail in.
FIRST:	Here, look at this. It's a bloody disgrace.
	Some idiot's put the hole in the wrong place!
	His arm won't reach.
SECOND:	Now what?
THIRD:	We'll stretch it, of course, you clot.
	Grab this rope – tie it on
	Then you can pull his arm along.
FIRST:	Blood and sand!
	Come on, why don't you give a hand?
SECOND:	Instead of just telling us what to do.
THIRD:	Well, I would if I could, but I'm older than you.
	[*Hammers in the second nail.*]
FIRST:	Now for his feet. Bloody hell!
	We'll have to stretch him here as well.
SECOND:	That hurt him bad.
FIRST:	We broke a vein – and snapped his sinews.

SECOND: He's in pain.
FIRST: Serves him right.
SECOND: You bet.
THIRD: Well, come on lads, we're not done yet.
FIRST: We can't lift that! It weighs a ton.
THIRD: Stop moaning – it's got to be done.
           Come on, grab hold – after three – Lift!
FIRST: It's heavy.
THIRD: Nearly there . . . steady . . . let it drop!
FIRST: Right – I'm knocking off.
SECOND: Yeah – time to stop.

           [*They sit and eat their lunch.*]

FIRST: Hey – you up there – want a drink?

           [*The SECOND SOLDIER hangs a notice on the cross: 'THIS IS JESUS,
           THE KING OF THE JEWS'.*]

SECOND: Here, you, King of the Jews, you with the crown.
           If you really are the son of God –
           Why don't you get down?
JESUS: ELOI ELOI LAMA SABACHTHANI
SECOND: What was that all about?
           What did he say?
FIRST: God knows! Come on – shall we call it a day?
THIRD: Aye – best be off before the light fails.
SECOND: Here – are we coming back tomorrow?
           Seems a shame to waste the nails.

           [*The SOLDIERS exit.*]

Unit 8

The Toodyay letters

Introduction and context

This unit is based around the fascinating discovery – in 1931 – of a sheaf of letters sent to a transported convict many years earlier by his wife back in England. The letters themselves are presented as a basis for an evocative performance project, focusing on the life of a particular convict and how the punishment inflicted upon him affected not only his life, but also that of his wife and family left behind.

In this unit, students will have the opportunity to engage in a sustained play-making project, based around the story of a real-life convict, William Sykes. Sykes was transported to Western Australia in 1865, the consequence of a poaching incident that went tragically wrong.

> Sykes lived in the village of Masborough, near Rotherham, in what is now South Yorkshire. One night, he and six other local men set out to poach a few rabbits from a nearby wood. A fight broke out when they were interrupted, and a gamekeeper was killed in the ensuing struggle. A reward was offered, and Sykes was informed on by another of the poachers eager to claim his £350 reward, then a huge sum. Sykes was soon arrested, tried for poaching and murder, and sentenced to penal servitude for life. As transportation to other parts of Australia had ceased by 1865, William Sykes was sent to the still sparsely populated region of Western Australia on board a transport ship. He was never again to see England, his wife Myra, or his four children Thirza, Ann, Alfred and William. He served out his term of imprisonment and died in 1891.
>
> We would never have known William Sykes' story but for the chance finding, in 1931, of a kangaroo skin pouch containing letters sent to him by his wife in Yorkshire. The pouch was found when the local police station in the town of Toodyay, where Sykes' few belongings were sent on his death, was demolished. The drama work is based around these letters, reprinted in Resource sheets 1 to 7 (pages 166–72). These provide a moving testimony to the hardship endured by William and his family, and their undying hope that one day they might be reunited.

The letters are explored from three different perspectives. In the first sequence of activities, the students are asked to consider using the reading of the letters themselves as a structural device. The representation of time and physical distance become central themes of the work as students create scenes that contrast the experiences and perspectives of the drama's main protagonists.

In the second sequence, William Sykes' story is divided into episodes that provide a basic structure for students' devising work. Working from captions, they explore the story primarily from William's perspective.

The third approach is based around a non-naturalistic dramatic device that allows students to experiment with *juxtaposition*, as scenes rapidly move across time and distance, unified once more by the central character of William Sykes himself.

Toodyay letters unit map

Activity	Description	Resources	Teacher notes
Introductory activity	Signs and symbols.	Collection of props	
Activity 1	Investigation of the Toodyay letters in groups.	Resource sheets 1–7	
Activity 2	Filling in the gaps in the correspondence. Staging the drama (approach 1) – letters structure.	Resource sheets 1–7	
Activity 3	Staging the drama (approach 2) – captions structure.	Resource sheets 1–7, 8	
Activity 4	Staging the drama (approach 3) – characters structure.	Resource sheets 1–7	

We anticipate that a group exploring all the activities in this unit would take about five one-hour lessons to complete the tasks.

To start the process, students are introduced to work on signs and symbols and their use in theatre.

Introductory activity

Signs and Symbols

A *sign* is an individual thing that creates meaning.

Signs create meaning in two basic ways:

- They have a literal meaning (they *denote* something).
- They may have a meaning beyond the literal (they *connote* something). (For instance a large, expensive car may connote far more about its owner than the fact that they need a means of transport!)

Symbols are particular kinds of signs: a symbol is a sign that in itself has no association with what we take it to mean – for example, scales can symbolise justice. In everyday life, signs and symbols are images or words used to convey information or meaning. They can include gestures as well as visual symbols: an outstretched hand or a pointing finger, or aural signs like cheering or booing.

Ask the class to list as many *signs* and *symbols* found in everyday life as they can. The list may include 'no entry' or 'one way' traffic signs or symbols such as those found on computer keyboards, trademarks or logos.

- *How do we know what the signs and symbols mean?*
- *Are there any signs that everyone on earth would understand, irrespective of culture?*

Signs and Symbols in Drama

In drama, everything that appears 'on stage' can be *read* by the audience as a sign. This is why mistakes on stage are sometimes *read* as deliberate – and why an actor with a cold may find that his hoarse voice is appraised as a significant factor in his characterisation. For this next section the teacher will need to accumulate a selection of props that might have 'symbolic' qualities – that might represent (*connote*) something beyond their 'everyday' use in the context of a drama. Some suggestions are:

- a quill pen and paper;
- a candle or oil lamp;
- a union flag ('Union Jack');
- a loaf of bread;
- a bible;
- an old spirit bottle;
- a locket or brooch;

- a broom;
- a bunch of keys;
- a pot of 'gold' coins;
- an axe;
- a pair of gold-rimmed spectacles;
- a scroll tied with ribbon

Place one of the objects in a particular area of the classroom, so that it is 'framed' or *on stage*. This could be achieved through lighting.

- Ask students to suggest a 'literal' meaning for the object (what it *denotes*).
- Ask them to suggest more symbolic or metaphorical possibilities. For instance, a broom may literally *denote* an object used for cleaning, but depending on the dramatic context may have *connotative* associations with *sweeping clean*, or with drudgery (or in another dramatic context, with witchcraft). In a particular drama, a pair of spectacles may have *connotative* associations with wisdom or old age, as well as denoting a device used to remedy poor eyesight!

Repeat the exercise with a number of objects. Try placing two or three objects together and asking the group to *read* the *stage picture* for possible meanings. Are there any objects that seem to 'naturally' go together? (In semiotics, signs that seem to 'belong' together are referred to as *codes*.)

If this group of objects made up part of the setting for the first scene of a drama, what would the audience be able to *read* about the drama's setting or characters? Ask the students, in groups of three or four, to create the title and basic scenario of the projected drama. Who are the main protagonists? What is the plot outline?

As the various approaches to dramatising the Toodyay letters unfold, encourage the students to experiment with the use of signs and symbols in their work. For instance, there will be opportunities for students to carefully select – and employ – props of the kind used in this exercise in order to deepen their work.

Activity 1

Divide the class into seven groups and give each group a copy of a letter to read. Ask them to record any sections that they find interesting or moving. After a suitable working period, ask each group to report back to the rest of the class:

- *Who is the letter for?*
- *Who wrote the letter?*
- *When was the letter written?*
- *What events does the letter describe?*
- *Are there any key lines or incidents that are particularly significant?*

After sharing the groups' responses, provide the context for the letters by telling the class the story of the kangaroo skin pouch and the letters it contained.

As the class reflect upon the story they have been told, what key questions or themes emerge from their initial engagement with the material? Discuss with the class any ideas that they have and record them – this will help shape the direction that the project might take. For example:

- *Was transportation a fair punishment for such a crime? Did the fact that William and his family were poor and hungry excuse his act in any way?*
- *How was it possible for William and Myra to sustain their hope to be reunited against such difficult circumstances?*
- *How did William survive on his own in a strange land?*
- *How did life change for Myra and the children? How did they endure the hardship that they must have suffered?*
- *How far do the letters reveal their real feelings?*

In the light of the work that they have undertaken earlier in this unit, are there any interesting symbols or metaphors suggested by the material? For example:

- What might the box – sent by Myra to William – symbolise? What of the objects within, like Alfred's 'little pocket knife'?
- What metaphors of loss – or hope – are evoked? For instance, Myra refers to William as the 'prodigal son' in one of the letters: what connotations does this phrase hold for the class?

Activity 2

Point out that the surviving letters are all sent to William in Australia from his family in England. There are, however, references (in letters two, four, five and six) to letters that William wrote back to his family in reply. In this sequence of activities, the students will begin to create fictional material by filling in the 'gaps' in the correspondence. They will then use the 'complete' sequence of letters as a basic dramatic structure.

First of all, allow the students time to study the particular letters that refer to William's replies. Give each group a different letter to 'investigate'.

According to letter number two, William wrote a letter to Myra whilst he was languishing in Portsmouth prison:

- *What kinds of things might William have written in his reply?*
- *What would he have wanted to tell his family?*
- *What clues do we have (in letter two) about Myra's state of mind, and the things she is most worried about? Would William refer to these, and perhaps seek to reassure her?*

Work through the other letters, encouraging the students to scrutinise them for the evidence they contain. As each group makes suggestions for possible content to be used in a 'reply', record them for future reference.

Once the process has been repeated for each group, suggest that they may now have enough ideas to begin drafting letters which William might have sent in reply to his wife at various points in the story. Because the letters do not in reality exist it may be interesting dramatically for the replies to survive only as fragments – perhaps they were 'damaged in transit' – or perhaps William simply didn't write very well. One simple method of drafting the replies would be to ask each student in a particular group to write just one or two sentences, which can then be assembled as a composite 'letter' consisting of unconnected fragments.

Once the sequence of letters and replies has been established, the task is to use the letters as a basic framework to stage the drama.

- What is the most appropriate physical layout for the stage in this drama?
- How can the two locations be represented? Is a 'naturalistic' setting appropriate for this drama or not?

- How might the students make use of choral effects – by 'layering' the reading of the letters to form a montage, or repeating them in the form of a cannon?
- How might the fragmentary form of the letters they create be reflected in the students' choice of dramatic form? Can they physicalise the disjointed nature of the writing?

The simplest structure might be to alternate the 'reading' of one letter (Myra and the children in Yorkshire) with its reply (William in prison or Australia). This would then allow the construction of short scenes interspersed between or during the letters – perhaps based on key passages in the various letters themselves or 'evoked' by the reading of the letters:

- What are the advantages of this structure for the construction of a play based on the story of William and Myra?
- Does the 'alternating' structure provide a means to explore the thoughts and feelings of both main characters?
- What opportunities does it provide for contrasting emotional moods, or for the creation of dramatic tension that might help keep an audience engaged?

Activity 3

A slightly different approach to dramatising the story would be to divide it into episodes, and to use these as the basis for a retelling of the story primarily from William's point of view. This could then be juxtaposed with dramatised episodes drawn from the letters that present the realities of life for his family in England.

Create six captions:

- Poaching
- Imprisonment
- The voyage
- Arrival
- Life in Australia (a significant or memorable incident)
- Last rites

Divide the class into six groups, and give each a caption on which to base a short scene. Again, the letters provide some clues as to possible content for these episodes, but the students themselves have opportunities here for imaginative work of their own construction. Remind them to employ their understanding of signs and symbols in this exercise.

Once the basic action of each scene is established ask the students to include dramatic devices that might help to explore William's own perspective:

- What are his thoughts and feelings at particular moments of the drama? (These could be presented as *thought tracking*, as *direct address* to the audience, or as *monologues*.)
- Does he make any friends in Australia? Can the students show something of William's character and state of mind by the way he relates to these 'significant others'?
- How does he live in Australia? How does it contrast with the way of life he might have been used to in England?
- What reminds him of home? For instance, could a symbolic object (perhaps something from the box sent from home) be particularly evocative for him?
- What about music? One of the transportation ballads encountered earlier in the unit, or a song about poaching such as *Rufford Park Poachers* (Resource sheet 8, page 173) might be used to good effect in the drama.

Once this basic structure is established, it may be fruitful to create other contrasting scenes, perhaps based upon imaginary or fictional encounters as well as incidents described or inferred by the letters. For instance:

- a scene where William is visited in prison by his family before his transportation;
- a scene which shows how all the objects sent to him in the box were chosen and acquired;
- a scene in which William dreams of his idealised family back in Yorkshire, contrasted with the reality;
- a 'fantasy' scene, showing the family reunited (which in reality, of course, did not take place).

The choice of these scenes is likely to depend upon the particular themes or questions – identified earlier – that most animate the class.

Structurally, this drama is likely to be slightly more complex than that suggested in Activity 1. A key concern in staging the drama may be in deciding whether the basic episodes need to be played in chronological order, or whether an alternative order is dramatically more effective.

- What advantages or disadvantages does this approach to creating a play give?
- By concentrating on William himself as the central character in this way, is it possible to balance 'psychological' concerns (his thoughts, feelings and aspirations) with the more 'social' and active orientation of the scenes created earlier?

Activity 4

A third possible approach to dramatising the letters develops further the notion of contrasting scenes played in juxtaposition. In this activity, the character of William Sykes is again the unifying element; he is seen both in the past – back in Yorkshire – and the 'present' of being a convict in Australia. Organise the class into groups of five or six. Ask each student to take on a role from the two sides of William's life, the 'reality' of the family prior to the poaching incident and the 'imagined reality' of life in Australia. Apart from the actor playing William, each member of the group must develop two characters – one from life before transportation and one from life in Australia.

The drama is made up of sequences of two scenes linked by a shared movement, gesture or phrase. For example, the first scene might depict William just before setting out on the poaching expedition, promising his family there will be 'meat on the table by the morning'. The action freezes as the actor playing Myra says, 'You're a good man, William.' The actors then move into a different position around William, as characters in a second scene from his future life in Australia. This scene begins with one of the characters uttering the lines, 'You're a good man, William' – perhaps intended ironically.

The resonance of the work might lie within the contrast of the characters and relationships played by the same actor, and in the contrast of the situations implied by the unifying phrase. Once the structure is established a range of characters and situations can be explored, and students have the opportunity to experiment with developing two contrasting characters and finding effective ways of playing the transition from one to the other.

- What opportunities does this structure provide for the 'manipulation' of time and place within the drama?
- How many different kinds of linking motifs – phrases, gestures or the use of props, for instance – can groups find to effectively connect their two scenes?

In experimenting with these three possible approaches to a theatre project based on the Toodyay letters, students will have opportunities to engage with the crucial issue of finding dramatic form suited to the rich content material. As they work, encourage them to experiment with the structural elements suggested, but also with ideas of their own. Remember that dramatic meaning is derived from the integration of form and content, and is 'constructed' by audiences: encourage the students to 'test out' their ideas in performance at every stage of the process. As Brecht reminds us, in theatrical matters 'the proof of the pudding' is always in the eating.

THE TOODYAY LETTERS

Resource sheet 1:   Transcriptions

Letter one, dated 15 March 1867, sent by Myra and the children to William whilst in prison in Portsmouth a month before he sailed to Australia

Dear Husband,

I write these few lines to you hoping to find you better than it leaves us at present. I have been very uneasy since you did not rite, my children cried when we got no leter. Mrs Bone [wife of another transported poacher] has got two letters since I got one. Will you please to rite to me and send me word how you are getting on. I have bilt myself up thinking I shal get to you sometime or another. My mother sends her best love to you. She has been very ill but she is better at present. We all send our kind love to you. We all regret very much for you, I hope there will be a righting for you yet. Woodhouse has been for giving himself up severl times when he has been in drink – I hope he will. We have wished scores of times that you were coming in to the house, we should squeeze you to death for we would like to see that . . . You must not delay riting if you can, it will ease my mind if you can. If ever it lays in your power to send for us when you get abroad I would freely sell all up to come to you if I possibly could.

Dear father do please writ to us. I sends one 100 kiss for you.
Thirza Sykes.

Ann Sykes sends Dear kisses. Father, I send a 100 kiss for you. Alfred sends kiss, kind love.

Love to you. Masbro'
Midland Road 33

THE TOODYAY LETTERS

Resource sheet 2: Transcriptions

Letter two, dated 19 March 1867, sent four days after the first letter

My dear Husband,

I have this afternoon received your letter and am glad to hear from you. I heard yesterday that there was a letter from you at Parkgate and wrote off immediately to the Governor of the Portsmouth prison asking him kindly send me word, if he could, what was the latest day I could see you, as I do not see how I could possibly undertake the journey this week, being without money.

If I had received your letter on Saturday, it was the reckoning [rent day] and I would have done my best to contrive it. But if you do not leave before the next reckoning I will come, if I come alone, for none of themselves are assisting me to do so either, so far. I feel it as much as you do to be very hard for you to be where you are and Woodhouse at liberty, but rest assured whether I get to see you or not I hope that when you arrive at your journey's end you will not forget us, for we are always thinking about you.

I hope the Governor will either send me a reply or allow you to do so, for I will leave no means untried to get to see you if there is time. But if I was at the expense, only to be too late when I got there, it will be a serious loss to me, situated as I am. I feel greatly hurt that you should send your letters to your brothers and sisters before me, for although we are separated there is no one I value and regard equal to you and I should like you to still have the same feeling toward me. If there is ever a chance of us being permitted to join you again even though it be a far-off land, both the children and myself will most gladly do so. Mr Bone [another poacher sentenced to transportation] has written to his wife to get the children's likeness taken for him to take away with him. I should like you to have ours if you are allowed the same privilige. Will you let me know? I cannot give you up. I live in the hope of our being together again somewhere before we end our days. My best love to you, the children also send their love to you, and remembrance from all friends.

Your affectionate wife Myra Sykes

THE TOODYAY LETTERS

Resource sheet 3:   Transcriptions

Letter three, dated 8 April 1867, sent as William is about to embark on the transport ship

My dear Husband

I have this day sent off a box for you which I hope you will receive safely. I have sent you all that I possibly could and am only sorry that it is not in my power to send you more. As soon as I received your letter I took it to Elizabeth [the eldest of William Sykes' three sisters]. She has sent you two of the smallest spice loaves, and gave me one shilling towards the expense. Then I went to Rebecca and she could not do anything towards it. Emma has sent the other spice loaf and mince pie, Elizabeth the testament and tract, and John the other two books. The remainder I have sent myself. I hope you will write back the very first opportunity to let me know if you have received it. [When] you write next send word whether a few postage stamps will be of any use to you. I walked to sheffield yesterday morning in the hope of getting a good shut-knife for you, but could not meet with any of them. If Saturday had been pay day I might have been able to get a trifle more for you. I called at John Cliffs, they sent their love to you and Mrs Cliffs sent an ounce of Tobacco. We also send our best love to you and the children all wish thet were going in the same ship as their Father. I have enclosed you a list of the articles in the box and M [mother] encloses a packet of needles with her respect. If you have the chance to earn any money in Australia you must save it all up and I will do the same, that if there is a chance of us rejoining you we may be able to do so. Be sure to write and let me know if you have received the box for I shall not be easy in my mind until I hear from you again. Remaining with best love and wishes for your welfare.

Your affectionate wife Myra Sykes

List of articles in the box
Three spice loaves – 2 pound cheese 2 pound sugar – 2 tea
Packet of spice – quire of paper
4 books – 1/2 dozen pipes
Bottle of Tobacco – Parcel of Tobacco
Old favourite Tobacco pouch
Thread needles, buttons, etcetera
Three bottles of ink and pens
2 fig cakes – Apples, oranges and lemons
Bottle of pickles – one and a quarter pounds bacon, flannel shirt, 1 belt, 2 flannel comforters, 1 hankerchief pocket, 2 caps, 2 purses, 1 comb, 2 cotton shirts and looking glass, 4 needles and thread, 6 hanks
Alfred sends his little pocket knife.

THE TOODYAY LETTERS

Resource sheet 4:   Transcriptions

Letter four, sent 20 September 1868

Dear Husband,

I take this opportunity of writing you these few lines to let you know that I received your letter dated 5th July 1868. Dear husband I was glad to hear that you were well and in good health. Mrs Bone had a letter and asked whether I had got one from you or not, and that put me about for I thought that something had happened to you because there was no letters for me. And I was much further I put about when I received your letter when it was a week amongst them [William Sykes' family] before I got it. Dear Husband when you write again send me word what sort of a passage you had when you were going out and send word whether you got that box I sent you when you were leaving this country, for you, never said in your letter whether you got it or not.

All send their love . . . Your daughter, Ann, is in place and is doing well and, Alfred is working in the mill and he gets 10 pence per day. Ann, Thirza, Alf and William send their kind love to you. William has got long white curly hair and he was not called William for nothing for he is a little rip right, and your brothers and sisters send their kind love to you. There was another fight over poaching with young Berdshaw last month. This took place on Lord Warncliff's estate. The Keeper was shot. Berdshaw's Father took it so much to heart that he went and threw himself on the rails and the trains past over him and killed him.

Dear Husband when you write again, direct your letter to Mrs Sykes, No 39 Midland Road, Masborough

THE TOODYAY LETTERS

Resource sheet 5:   Transcriptions

Letter five, dated 9 March 1872

Dear Husband,

I been long in writing to you, I hope you will forgive. I received your letter and was pleased with it. I think you might send me more word what you're doing. I hope this will find you in good health as it leaves us at present. I want you to send a line to Alfred. He is getting up, likes to go to the public, but is not a bad lad to me. I expect you will be a grandfather of two when this letter arrives. Ann is on again. She not had very good luck, lost a deal of time from being poorly but is looking well. My little Bill has been very poorly, he is better and looks well. It heartbreaks me to write like this. If the prodigal son could come back to his home once more there would be a rejoicing . . . And you mentioned about looking young. I thought you did when I saw you at Leeds. My heart broke nearly when I felt your hand being so soft. Dear Husband, you would be surprised to see what a great fine looking girl Thirza is. It will be my birthday on Tuesday, 17 of March. As for myself I am not looking very well at present. Brother and sister sends their best love to you. Alfred is in the Wombwell main pit with Ann's husband and my brother Ellis. Alfred works full week for nineteen and sixpence. He minds the engine. Ann's husband says he would work hard for you to come home if it could be done. My dear Husband I sends my nearest and dearest love to you, and all the children with a thousand loves and kiss wish we may meet again, Oh that we could in this world.

THE TOODYAY LETTERS

Resource sheet 6:   Transcriptions

Letter six, dated 11 April 1875

Dear Husband,

I write these few lines to you hoping to find you well as it leaves us at present. We received your letter dated 12th January and was glad to receive it . . . I don't doubt but that you wrote many letters that I never heard tell of. I once was three years and had not a letter . . . Your relations said that you was dead. I went to Rotherham Town Hall and asked whether you was dead or not. One of the police said he heard you was dead. I put the children and myself in black for you. My little Thirza went to the first place in deep black. Then I heard your sister Elizabeth had got a letter from you. My daughter Ann went to see if they had told her that you was all right and they told her that the letter had gone to sheffield and she could not see it. Husband, can't express myself to you but I hope to see you once more seated in the corner. I will be best for you if it comes to pass. Some days I feel pretty cheerful and others very sad, but I think it is owing to my age. Well, I must tell you that Ann getting for another and am sorry to tell you that he is not one of the best of Husbands. But Ann she would be cross with me if she knew I sent you word. I don' t think he is very fond of work – he is a unculted [uncultured] man. Dear Husband, I must tell you, my Alfred I believe is taller than you. People are surprised with him. Thirza, I believe she not far off eleven stone. William is a nice boy he does not lose an inch of his height. An would be cross with me if she knew I had sent you word.

Very best respects to you. My brothers and sisters send best love.

THE TOODYAY LETTERS

Resource sheet 7:   Transcriptions

Letter seven, 20 October 1875, from William's son, William Jnr

> *Dear Father,*
>
> *I write these few lines to find you better than it leaves us at present. My mother as been very ill and mesel I am a bit better. Dear Father, we think you have quite forgot us all. My sister Ann takes it hard at you not writing oftener. I must tell you that sister Ann as two nice boys. The oldest is a fine little fellow. Well, I must tell you what a stout young man my brother, Alfred as got and Thirza is a stout young woman. Poor Ann is very thin. Ann's husband and Alfred works at Aldwarke main pit . . . We don't live far from Aunt Rebecca. I often play with their little boy. My Aunt often say I am like my father . . . Dear father, you would hardly know Greasborough now if you seed it. We have got a new Congregational Church and I go to that school. Dear Father, Mother would like to know if they would allow you our likeness. Dear Father, you never name me in your letters but I can sit down and write a letter to you now. Dear Father, my mother wants to know if you ever hear of being set free.*
>
> *We all send kindest and dearest love to you and God bless you and thousand kisses for our dear Father from your Dear son,*
>
> *William.*

THE TOODYAY LETTERS

Resource sheet 8

Rufford Park Poachers – a traditional folk-song

A buck or doe believe it so
A pheasant or a hare
Were set on earth for everyone
Quite equal for to share

(Chorus) So poacher bold as I unfold
Keep up your gallant heart
And think about the poachers bold
That night in Rufford Park

They say that forty gallant poachers
They were in a mess
They'd often been attacked when
Their number it was less

All among the gorse to settle scores
These forty gathered stones
To make a fight for poor men's rights
And break those keepers' bones

The keepers went with flails against
The poachers and their cause
So no man there again would dare
To break the rich man's laws

All on the ground with a mortal wound
Head keeper Roberts lay
He never will rise up again
'Til the final judgement day

Of all that band who made a stand
To set a net or snare
Just four were brought before the court
And tried for murder there

The judge said 'For Roberts' death
Transported you must be
To serve a term of fourteen years
In convict slavery'

So poacher bold, your tale is told
Keep up your gallant heart
And think about those poachers bold
That night in Rufford Park

Bibliography

Adshead, K. (2001) *The Bogus Woman*, London: Oberon Books

Amnesty International (September 2003). Online. Available HTTP:<http://refuge.amnesty.org/htm/home.htm>

Arts Council of Great Britain (1992) *Drama in Schools*, London: ACGB

Arts Council England (2003) *Drama in Schools* (second edition), London: ACGB

Axelrod, T. (2001) *Hans and Sophie Scholl – German Resisters of the White Rose*, New York: The Rosen Publishing Group

Barba, E. (1994) *The Paper Canoe*, London: Routledge

Belbin, R.M. (1981) *Management Teams*, Oxford: Butterworth Heinemann

Bennett, S. (1997) *Theatre Audiences*, London: Routledge

Berkoff , S. (1981) *Metamorphosis*, London: Amber Lane Press

Berkoff, S. (1990) Interview for Japanese Television; *Salomé* videotape, British Theatre Museum, in Rosen, C. (2000) Ph.D. Thesis. Online. Available HTTP:<http://www.iainfisher.com/sbdisa5.html>

Boal, A. (1979) *Theatre of the Oppressed*, London: Pluto Press

Bolton, G. (1998) *Acting in Classroom Drama – A Critical Analysis*, Stoke on Trent: Trentham Books

Bolton, G. (2000) 'It's All Theatre' in *Drama Research* Vol. 1, April 2000; National Drama Publications

Brunvand, J.H. (1981) *The Vanishing Hitchhiker – American Urban Legends and their Meaning*, New York: W.W. Norton & Co.

Cawley, A.C. (ed.) (1956) *Everyman and Medieval Miracle Plays*, London: J.M. Dent and Sons

Clark, M.S. (1989) *Letters to George: The Account of a Rehearsal*, London: Nick Hern Books

Department for Education and Science (1988) *The Education Reform Act*, London: HMSO

Department for Education and Science (1989) *The Education (National Curriculum) (Attainment Targets and Programmes of Study in English)*, London: HMSO

Department for Education and Employment (DfEE) (2000) *Developing a Global Dimension in the School Curriculum*, London: DfEE Publications

Eisner, E.W. (1994) *Educational Imagination: On the Design and Evaluation of School Programs*, (third edition), New York: Macmillan

Eisner, E. (1995) *The Art of Educational Evaluation: A Personal View*, London: Falmer Press

Esslin, M. (1987) *The Field of Drama*, London: Methuen

Fleming, M. (1994) *Starting Drama Teaching*, London: David Fulton

Fleming, M. (1997) *The Art of Drama Teaching*, London: David Fulton

Fleming, M. (2001) *Teaching Drama in Primary and Secondary Schools*, London: David Fulton

Fyfe, H. (2001) 'Broadening the Base' in *Drama Research* Vol. 2, May 2001, National Drama Publications

Garrett-Groag, L. (1998) *The White Rose*, New York: The Dramatists Play Service

Gellately, R. (2001) *Backing Hitler – Consent and Coercion in Nazi Germany*, Oxford: OUP

Hasluck, A. (1959) *Unwilling Emigrants*, Oxford: OUP

Hornbrook, D. (1989) *Education and Dramatic Art*, Oxford: Basil Blackwell

Hornbrook, D. (1991) *Education in Drama – Casting the Dramatic Curriculum*, London: Falmer Press

Hornbrook, D. (1998a) *Education and Dramatic Art*, (second edition), London: Routledge

Hornbrook, D. (1998b) *On the Subject of Drama*, London: Routledge

Hughes, R. (1996) *The Fatal Shore*, London: The Harvill Press

Kemp, A. and Ashwell, M. (2000) *Progression in Secondary Drama*, Oxford: Heinemann

Kirby, M. (1987) *A Formalist Theatre*, Philadelphia: University of Pennsylvania Press

Lacey, S. and Woolland, B. (1992) 'Educational Drama and Radical Theatre Practice' in *New Theatre Quarterly* Vol. VIII, No. 29, February 1992, Cambridge: CUP

Leach, P. (undated manuscript) *Original Sin* (unpublished play)

Lucas, B. (2001) 'Creative Teaching, Teaching Creativity and Creative Learning' in Craft, A., Jeffrey, B. and Leibling, M. (eds) *Creativity in Education*, London: Continuum

Mertus, J., Tesanovic, J., Metikos, H. and Bovic, R. (1997) *The Suitcase – Refugee Voices from Bosnia and Croatia*, Berkeley, California: UCP

Morgan, N. and Saxton, J. (1987) *Teaching Drama – A Mind of Many Wonders*, London: Hutchinson

National Advisory Committee on Creative and Cultural Education (NACCCE) (1999) *All Our Futures: Creativity, Culture and Education*, London: DfEE

National Curriculum Council (1990) *The Arts 5–16: A Curriculum Framework*, London: HMSO

Neelands, J. (1994) 'Drama Without Walls – Alternative Aesthetics in Educational Drama' in *Drama – One Forum Many Voices* Vol. 2, No. 2, spring 1994

Neelands, J. (1998) *Beginning Drama 11–14*, London: David Fulton

Neelands, J. (2000) *Structuring Drama Work* (second edition), Cambridge: CUP

New Zealand Ministry of Education (September 2003) *Assessment Exemplars – The Drama Matrix* (draft). Online. Available HTTP:<http://www.tki.org.nz/r/assessment/exemplars/arts/drama/drama_matrix_e.html>

Nicholson, H. (ed.) (2000) *Teaching Drama 11–18*, London: Continuum

O'Neill, C. (1995) *Drama Worlds – A Framework for Process Drama*, Portsmouth NH: Heinemann US

O'Toole, J. (1992) *The Process of Drama*, London: Routledge

O'Toole, J. and Haseman, B. (1988) *Dramawise – An Introduction to GCSE Drama*, Oxford: Heinemann

Peukert, D. (1993) *Inside Nazi Germany – Conformity, Opposition and Racism in Everyday Life*, London: Penguin

Qualifications and Curriculum Authority (2002) *Creativity: Find it, Promote it*, London: QCA

Refugee Council (2002a) *Information In-depth – A Refugee Council Information Pack*, London: Refugee Council

Refugee Council (2002b) *Information – Refugees Are People Like . . .* , London: Refugee Council

Refugee Council (2002c) *A Refugee Council Information Pack – Schools Information Pack – Under 11 year olds*, London: Refugee Council

Refugee Council (2002d) *A Refugee Council Information Pack – Schools Information Pack – 11–18 Year Olds*, London: Refugee Council

Refugee Council (2003) *Information – Nailing Press Myths about Refugees*, London: Refugee Council

Refugee Council (September 2003) Online. Available HTTP:<http://www.refugeecouncil.org.uk/ contact/ cont003.htm>

Rose, M. (ed.) (1961) *The Wakefield Mystery Plays*, London: Evans Brothers Ltd

Schechner, R. (1985) *Between Theatre and Anthropology*, Philadelphia: University of Pennsylvania Press

Schechner, R. (1988) *Performance Theory*, London: Routledge

Schechner, R. (1993) *The Future of Ritual*, London: Routledge

Scholl, I. (1983) *The White Rose – Munich 1942–1943*, Hanover NH: Wesleyan University Press

Seal, G. (September 2003) *A Kangaroo Skin Pouch of Letters*. Online. Available HTTP:<http://simply australia.mountaintracks.com.au/issue5/TOODYAY_LETTERS_2.html>

Seltzer, V. and Bentley, T. (1999) *The Creative Age: Knowledge and Skills for the New Economy*, London: Demos

Swift, J. (ed. Heilman, R.) (1969/1726) *Gulliver's Travels*, New York: Modern Library

Taylor, D. (September 2003) *William Sykes*. Online. Available HTTP:<http://website.lineone.net/ ~bill.sykes/>

Toye, N. and Prendiville, F. (2000) *Drama and Traditional Story for the Early Years*, London: RoutledgeFalmer

Thompson, J. (1999) *Drama Workshops for Anger Management and Offending Behaviour*, London: Jessica Kingsley Publishers

von Glasersfeld, E. (1989) 'Constructivism in Education' in Husen, T. and Postlewaite, N. (eds), *International Encyclopedia of Education* [Suppl.], (pp.162–163), Oxford: Pergamon Press

Wigan LEA (2002) *Arts Reasoning and Thinking Skills*, Wigan: Wigan Council Department of Education

Index

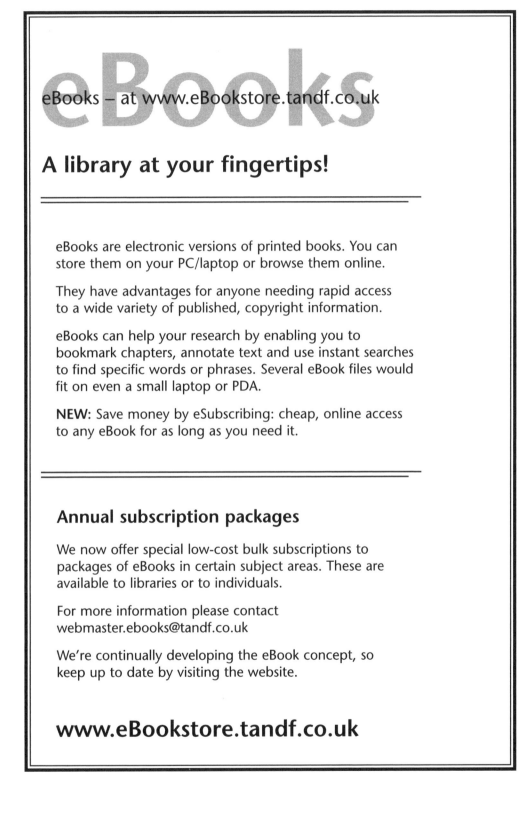